GAME DAY
OKLAHOMA FOOTBALL

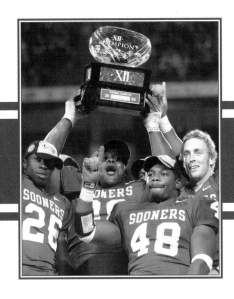

GAME DAY
OKLAHOMA FOOTBALL

**The Greatest Games, Players, Coaches and Teams
in the Glorious Tradition of Sooner Football**

TRIUMPH
B O O K S
CHICAGO

Athlon® Sports™
AMERICA'S PREMIER SPORTS ANNUALS

Library of Congress Control Number: 2006902918

This book is available in quantity at special discounts for your group or organization. For further information, contact:

Triumph Books
542 South Dearborn Street
Suite 750
Chicago, Illinois 60605
(312) 939-3330
Fax (312) 663-3557

CONTRIBUTING WRITER: George Schroeder

EDITOR: Rob Doster

PHOTO EDITOR: Tim Clark
PHOTO ASSISTANT: Danny Murphy

DESIGN: Anderson Thomas Design
PRODUCTION: Odds & Ends Multimedia

PHOTO CREDITS: Athlon Sports Archive, Univerity of Oklahoma, AP/Wide World Photos, Getty Images, Jerry Laizure, Lisa Hall, John Williamson

Printed in U.S.A.

ISBN-13: 978-1-57243-883-5
ISBN-10: 1-57243-883-5

CONTENTS

Jason White

Foreword

Sooner born and Sooner bred—when I die I'll be Sooner dead. Growing up in Tuttle, Oklahoma, I heard that saying a lot. Tuttle is a small farming community about 25 miles west of Norman, Oklahoma. I grew up thinking that the University of Oklahoma was the only college around because it was so close to home, and it was all most everyone in Tuttle ever talked about. There wasn't much to do growing up, so I got into sports at an early age. I started playing football when I was in the first grade, and that's when I really started to realize that the Sooners were a big deal. When I would go to practice everyone would be wearing some sort of Sooner apparel, or they would want to be the same number as their favorite Sooner. As I got older, and the more I got into watching the Sooners on TV, the bigger the dream became to me. The dream I am talking about was playing college football. At the time it was just playing—for any team—but as I got older, I wanted to play for the Sooners. I always imagined what it would be like to play for the team right down the road.

As I continued to progress in football during my high school years, I could see that my dream might become reality. I will never forget the moment I was watching Coach Stoops being announced as the new head coach. I was not heavily recruited by the Sooners until Coach Stoops stepped in. The energy that he brought to the football program caused me to be even more excited to play football for the University of Oklahoma. The night after my recruiting trip to the University of Oklahoma, I committed to play for the Sooners.

The moment I stepped foot on campus, I was overwhelmed by the tradition of the program. Walking down the halls of the Switzer Center gave me a glance of the past teams, players, and coaches: Steve Owens, Billy Sims, Bud Wilkinson, Brian Bosworth, Barry Switzer, Joe Washington, Jack Mildren, to name a few. I could go on for days about the great players and coaches of the Sooners. I soon realized that I was playing for a team with one of the greatest traditions in college football.

I could not have handpicked a better coach to play for than Bob Stoops. Coach Stoops really emphasized the tradition of Oklahoma football. Coach would randomly show us clips of past teams and bring in players from the past to speak to us. These are guys that I heard my dad talk about when I was a kid, and now they were standing right in front of me. Hearing these guys talk about the amount of pride, hard work, and dedication they put into the program made me want to work harder to continue the tradition of the Sooners. Playing for a program with such great tradition ensured the team was always in a position to compete for a Big 12 championship and a national championship. During my career, I was fortunate enough to be a part of three Big 12 championships and a national championship.

Now that my playing days are behind me, I have since gained a greater appreciation for the things our team accomplished and all the awards my teammates and I received. To have been part of an era during which Oklahoma football climbed back to the top and the memories that I have from playing football at the University of Oklahoma are priceless; however, the bond that I now share with past, present and future players at Oklahoma will always be what I appreciate most about playing for the University of Oklahoma.

—Jason White

Jason White in 2005 with a Heisman football autographed by all living Heisman Trophy winners. He donated the football to a charity auction.

Adrian Peterson

Introduction

The images are unforgettable and too numerous to count. The dominant teams of Bud Wilkinson, which reeled off historic winning streaks of 31 and 47 games. The unstoppable wishbone offense of Barry Switzer, with maestros like Jamelle Holieway directing the action and great backs like Greg Pruitt, Joe Washington and Billy Sims running to glory. Unforgettable tilts with Texas and Nebraska. National championships won, legends created.

Since the second half of the 20th century began, no college football program—not Notre Dame, not Alabama, not Miami, not USC—can claim as much gridiron success as the Oklahoma Sooners. And with Bob Stoops at the helm and players like Adrian Peterson still eager to wear the crimson and cream, the Sooners show no signs of slowing anytime soon.

The pageantry and drama of Oklahoma football have been distilled into the pages that follow. It's a daunting task, as few college football programs in the country inspire the loyalty and passion that the Sooner football program exacts from its fans—and with good reason.

Through the words and images we present, you'll get a taste of what Sooner football is all about. Decades have passed since players first donned those crimson jerseys, but one thing hasn't changed: Oklahoma football is an unmatched tradition, a legacy of greatness, a way of life in the Sooner State.

TRADITIONS AND PAGEANTRY

They travel from all over the state, flying flags and honking horns. On autumn weekends, crimson-clad fans stream into Norman. They gather in the old stadium, where pride and tradition intersect. As James Garner, the actor who is a Norman native and lifelong OU fan, says during the pregame introductions: "THIS is Oklahoma football!"

——— The Colors ———

The distinctive crimson and cream were chosen more than a century ago by a committee formed for the purpose. Led by Miss May Overstreet, the only woman faculty member at the time, the committee hit upon the winning color scheme. After an initial display on a platform during an assembly, the student body approved.

Although the colors may have evolved to red and white, the official colors—and the colors of the football helmet and jersey reflect this—are crimson and cream.

1

The Nickname

The nickname "Sooner" has its base in the history of Oklahoma—the territory and then the state. In 1889, the U.S. government opened the Oklahoma Territory to settlers with a now-legendary land run. Land was free to anyone who would stake their claim, and settlers from the world over arrived to grab their share.

There were few rules. One of those rules was that settlers were required to start the race at the same time, with a cannon's blast used to signal the start of the land run.

The settlers who started on time were known as "Boomers." A sizable contingent, however, got an early start, breaking the rules. They were known as "Sooners."

Oklahoma became known as the Sooner State. And the term *Sooner* soon came to be associated with a can-do spirit that pervaded the land.

OU's teams were first known as Rough Riders or Boomers. But around 1908, they were tagged as Sooners, a shortening of the name of an athletic booster club known as the Sooner Rooters.

They've been known as Sooners ever since.

The Sooner Schooner

Pulled by ponies Boomer and Sooner, OU's distinctive Sooner Schooner is one of college football's most recognizable mascots. Introduced in 1964, it didn't become an official mascot until 1980—but it had long since become a familiar staple of OU football games.

The Sooner Schooner is a replica of the Conestoga (covered) wagons so often used for transportation by the pioneers who first staked their claims in Oklahoma. Piloted by a member of the Ruf-Neks spirit group—Mick Cottom, a freshman from Liberty Mounds, Oklahoma, was the first, way back in 1964—the Sooner Schooner races onto Owen Field after Sooner scores.

The Sooner Schooner and the ponies are housed in Sapulpa, Oklahoma, at the Bartlett Ranch. Charley F. "Buzz" Bartlett and his brother, Dr. M.S. Bartlett, donated the original Sooner Schooner and the ponies.

The original Sooner Schooner has been retired but is prominently displayed in the student union.

—— Boomer and Sooner ——

Fuzzier two-legged counterparts to the real ponies, the costumed mascots Boomer and Sooner were introduced to OU fans in August 2005. Wearing OU football uniforms, the friendly horses are hits with the children.

—— Mex the Dog ——

From 1915 to 1928, Mex the Dog fired up the faithful. The canine roamed the sidelines at OU football and baseball games, wearing a red sweater with the letter O. His most important role was to prevent stray dogs from wandering onto the field.

Mex was adopted in 1914 by U.S. Army medic Mott Keys, who was deployed to Mexico during the Mexican Revolution unrest. When Keys, a native of Hollis, Oklahoma, later attended OU, he took Mex with him. And the canine quickly became a fan favorite; legend has it that his barks accompanied touchdowns and home runs.

Mex gained fame beyond OU in 1924. After the Sooners lost to Drake, he didn't make the train home. According to Sooner lore, Mex planned to avenge the loss by attacking the Drake Bulldogs. After a 50¢ reward was offered, Mex was found at the Arkansas City, Kansas, train station.

He attended the next week's game.

When Mex died in 1928, the university closed for his funeral. He is buried somewhere beneath the existing stadium.

The Ruf-Neks

Formed in 1915, the Ruf-Neks are an unofficial spirit group that has long been part of OU's game-day culture. The Ruf-Neks are the official caretakers of the Sooner Schooner and its ponies. Wearing distinctive uniforms—red button-down shirts and white pants—they patrol the sidelines at home games with shotguns and paddles.

Their boisterous image came honestly. Way back in 1915, a group of rowdy OU students was chastised by an older woman seated behind them in the stands.

"Sit down and be quiet, you roughnecks!" she scolded.

Needless to say, the Ruf-Neks haven't sat or turned down the volume since.

The Pride of Oklahoma

For almost a century, OU football has been accompanied and encouraged by the sounds of the Pride of Oklahoma Marching Band. It had its roots as a pep band; beginning in 1901, students and Norman residents combined to form an informal band. The first student band was formed in 1904 by Lloyd Curtis.

Today the Pride of Oklahoma boasts 300 members. Although the school's fight song "Boomer Sooner" is the Pride's most recognizable tune—and with good reason, as it is played at every opportunity and to end each and every band rehearsal—the band has become known for its musical excellence as well.

The band is known for intricate and creative marching patterns. But many fans still thrill to see one of its most simple: the interlocking "OU" that marches downfield during pregame festivities, accompanied by "Boomer Sooner."

The Seed Sower

Standing proudly near the edge of the South Oval on the main campus, the Seed Sower statue is one of OU's most recognizable symbols. The Seed Sower, which also graces the official university seal, stands for a parable told by David Ross Boyd, the university's first president, about a seed sower planting the seeds of knowledge.

But it has also become a part of OU football tradition. When the Sooners learn their bowl destination, the statue on the South Oval routinely receives fresh adornment. For example, when OU went to the Orange Bowl all those years in the Big 8—and again in 2000 and 2004—the statue's sack of seeds was filled with fresh oranges.

Gaylord Family–Oklahoma Memorial Stadium

One of the 15 largest on-campus stadiums, Gaylord Family–Oklahoma Memorial Stadium is often simply referred to as Owen Field, which was its original name. With a capacity of 82,112, it features state-of-the-art facilities while retaining the look and feel of the historic venue it is.

The first game was played at the site in 1923—fittingly, a 63–7 win over Washington of Missouri. The field was named after coach Bennie Owen, who coached the Sooners when the stadium was constructed.

The original plans called for a combination stadium and student union; the union was later built separately, a few hundred yards to the northwest. But beginning in 1925, when the original west-side stands were constructed, Owen Field stood proudly on the eastern edge of the heart of campus. Seating 16,000, it was renamed Oklahoma Memorial Stadium—to honor OU students and staff who died in World War I.

When east-side stands were added in 1929, the capacity increased to 32,000. Over the years, the venerable stadium has been refurbished and expanded several times. In 1949, the north end was enclosed, giving the stadium its distinctive U-shape. In 1975, the west-side upper deck and new press box was added, pushing capacity to 71,187. The south end zone was added in 1980, bringing capacity to 75,004.

The latest renovation and expansion came with the new century, a $65 million east-side

upper-deck project that added 8,000 seats. Completed in 2003, the state-of-the-art addition features 54 luxury suites and an extensive stadium-club section.

At that time, the stadium was renovated with the addition of a rich, red brick façade, helping enhance the traditional ambiance. The stadium was renamed in honor of the Gaylord family of Oklahoma City, which contributed millions to the athletics department and for academic pursuits at OU.

From 1970 through 1993, the Sooners played on artificial turf—it sure seemed those Wishbone scatbacks were faster on that slippery surface, didn't it? Natural grass was reinstalled in 1994.

"Boomer Sooner"

The song is simple but unmistakable. The lyrics were composed in 1905 by OU student Arthur M. Alden. The tune was borrowed from Yale University's "Boola Boola." The second half of the song's lyrics were borrowed from North Carolina's "I'm a Tar Heel Born." But the result is all Oklahoma and known nationwide.

Boomer Sooner, Boomer Sooner

Boomer Sooner, Boomer Sooner

Boomer Sooner, Boomer Sooner

Boomer Sooner, OK U!

Oklahoma, Oklahoma

Oklahoma, Oklahoma

Oklahoma, Oklahoma

Oklahoma, OK U!

I'm a Sooner born and Sooner bred

And when I die, I'll be Sooner dead

Rah Oklahoma, Rah Oklahoma

Rah Oklahoma, OK U!

"The OU Chant"

Written in 1936 by Jessie Lone Clarkson Gilkey, director of the OU girls' glee club, the OU Chant is played as fans, students, athletes and alumni stand and raise one finger in the air. The gesture shows unity of all those who are Sooners.

O-K-L-A-H-O-M-A

Our chant rolls on and on!

Thousands strong

Join heart and song

In alma mater's praise

Of Campus beautiful by day and night

Of colors proudly gleaming Red and White

'Neath a western sky

OU's chant will never die.

Live on University!

"Oklahoma!"

The Pride of Oklahoma often plays the rousing state song, which was the chorus of Rodgers and Hammerstein's *Oklahoma!*

Oklahoma, where the wind comes sweepin' down the plain

And the wavin' wheat can sure smell sweet

When the wind comes right behind the rain.

Oklahoma, Ev'ry night my honey lamb and I

Sit alone and talk and watch a hawk

Makin' lazy circles in the sky.

We know we belong to the land

And the land we belong to is grand!

And when we say:

Ee-ee-ow! A-yip-i-o-ee-ay!

We're only sayin',

You're doin' fine, Oklahoma!

Oklahoma, O-K!

O-K-L-A-H-O-M-A!

Brian Bosworth

THE GREATEST PLAYERS

Four Heisman winners. One hundred forty-one All-Americans. Countless all-conference types (Okay, 416). The point is, the list of Sooner greats goes on and on. The only problem when talking about them is, how do you rank them? And where do you stop? Here are a few of the many who have etched their names into Sooner lore.

BRIAN BOSWORTH
Linebacker, 1984–1986

The antics of "the Boz" were unforgettable. The multicolored Mohawk. The off-beat comments. The suspension for steroids. The T-shirt: National Communists Against Athletes. The flamboyant sideshow sometimes hides the substance: Brian Bosworth was one of the best linebackers in OU history. A two-time winner of the Butkus Award, Bosworth was a devastating defender. He led OU in tackles in each of his three seasons—tallying 133, 144 and 136 tackles. OU won the national championship in 1985. Here is something else you might not have known: the Boz was an Academic All-American in 1986. Of course, the same guy tested positive for steroids a short time later, missed the 1987 Orange Bowl and left school a year early for the NFL. He played three seasons for the Seattle Seahawks, but his career was finished by a shoulder injury.

PAUL "BUDDY" BURRIS
Guard, 1946–1948

Buddy Burris—the first of five talented brothers to play for OU—was the Sooners' first three-time All-American. The Muskogee, Oklahoma, native might have been limited only by the rule that prevented freshmen from playing; once he stepped into the lineup as a sophomore, he made a sizable impact on both the offensive and defensive lines. Burris was known for opening huge holes for OU's running backs. Defensively, he chased ball carriers all over the field. He finished his career by helping start a 31-game winning streak. A ninth-round draft choice by Brooklyn in 1949, Burris was later inducted into the Helms Athletic Foundation Football Hall of Fame.

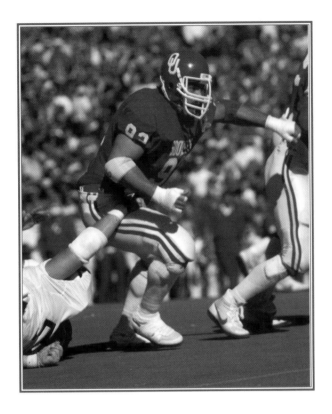

TONY CASILLAS
Defensive Tackle, 1982–1985

One of the best ever at a position that has been well-stocked at OU, Tony Casillas was dominating from his noseguard position. Barry Switzer once called him perhaps the best defensive lineman to play at OU—and remember, a guy named Lee Roy Selmon looms over all Sooner D-linemen. A two-time All-American (1984 and 1985), Casillas helped lead OU to the 1985 national championship. That year, despite nearly constant double-teams, he had 55 tackles and two sacks. A year earlier, Casillas had 88 tackles, including 21 for loss—and 10 sacks—and was named the Big 8's defensive player of the year. Casillas was the No. 2 overall selection in the 1986 NFL Draft and went on to a 13-year career. He has been elected to the College Football Hall of Fame.

JOSH HEUPEL
Quarterback, 1999–2000

He came out of nowhere—okay, from Snow Junior College—and began flinging passes everywhere. A coach's son from South Dakota, Josh Heupel was the single-most important player in OU's surge back into the national spotlight. Efficiently running the spread offense brought in by new coach Bob Stoops, Heupel took the Sooners to their first bowl game in five seasons in 1999. A year later, Heupel took the Sooners to the national championship. Along the way, he became an All-American and was the runner-up for the Heisman Trophy. In only two years at OU, Heupel forever embedded himself in Sooner lore. He finished as OU's career passing leader (7,456 yards), career TD passes leader (53) and career 300-yard passing games leader (14). An injury cut short any chance Heupel had of playing in the NFL, and he went into coaching. Heupel was hired in December 2005 as OU's quarterbacks coach, replacing Chuck Long (who went to San Diego State as head coach).

KEITH JACKSON
Tight End, 1984–1987

Keith Jackson was lured to OU by Barry Switzer's pitch that he was ditching the wishbone in favor of a passing attack. Instead, when Troy Aikman was injured (he later transferred to UCLA), the Sooners went back to the wishbone. And the extraordinarily gifted tight end from Little Rock, Arkansas, found himself as a tight end in an offense that didn't pass very often. At 6'3", 242 pounds, Jackson was fast, with great hands. He found a niche as a big-play threat, sometimes on reverses. In 1986, OU attempted 7.3 passes per game. In 1987, OU attempted 8.7 passes per game. Jackson was an All-American both years. In OU's win over Penn State in the 1986 Orange Bowl—which gave the Sooners the national championship—Jackson caught a touchdown pass, outrunning a safety for a 71-yard score. The 13th player selected in the first round of the NFL Draft, Jackson played with the Philadelphia Eagles and Green Bay Packers; he

was the NFL's Rookie of the Year in 1988, when he had 81 catches—19 more than his career total at OU. Jackson won a Super Bowl with the Packers. He was elected to the College Football Hall of Fame in 2001. Jackson now lives in his hometown of Little Rock, where he works with his charity, Positive Atmosphere Reaches Kids.

TOMMY MCDONALD
Halfback, 1954–1956

During Tommy McDonald's time at Oklahoma, the Sooners never lost a football game. And he was a big reason for that. Small (5'9", 147 pounds) but super-quick, the kid from Albuquerque, New Mexico, was a spark plug for much of OU's 47-game winning streak. McDonald finished third in Heisman balloting in 1956 and was named the winner of the Maxwell Award and *The Sporting News*' college Player of the Year. This despite playing only about half of each game in Bud Wilkinson's platoon system—and because OU was so often so far ahead of opponents that the starters didn't see much second-half action. McDonald played 12 years in the NFL with the Eagles, Rams, Falcons, Cowboys and Browns. Though he started his career as a halfback, he made his name as a wide receiver. In 1962, he was a *Sports Illustrated* coverboy, touted as having pro football's best hands. McDonald was elected to the College Football Hall of Fame in 1985 and the Pro Football Hall of Fame in 1998, becoming the second Sooner to be so honored.

JACK MILDREN
Quarterback, 1969-1971

In 1971, when OU featured one of the best offensive teams in college football history, Mildren was the catalyst. The Abilene, Texas, native didn't come to OU to run the wishbone, but when offensive coordinator Barry Switzer junked the veer offense three games into the 1970 season, installing the newfangled attack, Mildren proved an able pitch man. He was fast (4.6-second 40-yard dash), with a strong arm—perfect for the offense. There were growing pains. But by 1971, the Sooners had settled in.

Mildren rushed for 1,289 yards and 20 touchdowns. He threw for 889 yards and 10 touchdowns. OU averaged 469.9 rushing yards, 556.8 total yards and 44.5 points per game. All three averages led the nation. Mildren was named an All-American, matching his status in the classroom. Mildren served as Oklahoma's lieutenant governor from 1990 to 1994, and is now a radio personality.

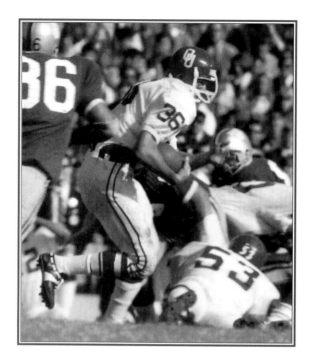

STEVE OWENS
Running Back, 1967–1969

They just kept feeding Steve Owens the football. He just kept on bulling ahead, piling up the yards. And that was how the kid from Miami, Oklahoma, won the Heisman Trophy. Owens set NCAA records for touchdowns (57) and carries (958) in a three-year career. As a senior in 1969, Owens rushed for 1,523 yards and 23 touchdowns and edged Purdue's Mike Phipps to win college football's most coveted award. But a year earlier, Owens had rushed for 1,649 yards and 21 touchdowns. Five days after winning the Heisman, Owens carried an amazing 55 times for 261 yards and two touchdowns as OU edged Oklahoma State 28–27. Owens finished with 4,041 career yards and set 13 school records, nine Big 8 records and seven NCAA marks. He was elected to the College Football Hall of Fame in 1991, served as OU's athletics director from 1996 to 1998 and remains one of the most active former Heisman winners in promoting that organization.

ADRIAN PETERSON
Running Back, 2004–present

It's not customary to include a player whose eligibility hasn't yet expired—and especially a running back at a school with such history at the position. But Peterson is special. As a freshman in 2004, he lived up to his recruiting billing as the best high school player in the nation when he rushed for 1,925 yards—an NCAA freshman record and an OU single-season record—and finished as the Heisman Trophy runner-up. That was the highest-ever finish by a freshman in the long history of college football's most prestigious award. Although Peterson missed part or all of four games in 2005 because of injury, he still rushed for more than 1,100 yards. As the 2006 season neared, he was perhaps the leading candidate for the Heisman.

GREG PRUITT
Running Back/Halfback, 1970–1972

Another in a long line of great Sooner running backs, Greg Pruitt benefited from OU's switch to the wishbone during the 1970 season. He had been a wide receiver, but was moved to halfback when then–offensive coordinator Barry Switzer switched to the 'bone three games into the season. Good move. Pruitt moved into the starting lineup and became a two-time All-American. In 1971, Pruitt wore a T-shirt that said "Hello" on the front and "Good-bye" on the back. But it's not boasting if you can back it up, and he did. Barry Switzer had given the shirt to Pruitt. Pruitt rushed for 1,665 yards that season, averaging a then–NCAA record 9.1 yards per carry. He finished third in the Heisman Trophy balloting. A year later, despite a late-season injury, Pruitt finished second (to Nebraska's Johnny Rodgers) in the Heisman voting. A second-round pick by the Cleveland Browns, Pruitt made the Pro Bowl four times in a 12-year career. He finished with 13,000 all-purpose yards. Pruitt was inducted into the College Football Hall of Fame in 1999.

DARRELL ROYAL
Quarterback/Defensive Back, 1946–1949

Even OU fans perhaps know him best as Texas's legendary head coach. But before he led the Longhorns to prominence, Darrell Royal was a Sooner standout. The Hollis, Oklahoma, native was considered extraordinarily versatile, even in an era when versatility was routine. He punted superbly, played halfback and quarterback exquisitely and was a pretty fair defensive back—Royal still owns OU's interceptions record, with 18. One of his greatest moments came in 1949, when his late touchdown pass to end Jim Owens gave OU a 20–14 win over Texas. Royal went on to a 20-year career as head coach at Texas that included two national championships and 11 Southwest Conference championships. Unfortunately, he was 12–7–1 against OU.

Lee Roy Selmon, 1975 Lombardi Award winner

LEE ROY SELMON
Defensive Tackle, 1972–1975

Legend has it that Lee Roy Selmon was never knocked to the ground while playing for OU. Not once. And with the talent he possessed, that tale might not be too tall. Quite simply, Selmon is considered by most to be the best OU player, ever. At 6'2" and 256 pounds, he was the youngest of three All-America brothers from Eufaula, Oklahoma, who played for OU. In 1973, Lee Roy, Lucious and Dewey all started on the Sooners' defensive line. Against archrival Nebraska that year, OU won 27–0—and the Huskers did not run a play in Sooner territory. But there was no doubt as to which Selmon was the best. A two-time All-American, Lee Roy won the Outland Trophy and Lombardi Award. In 1975, he finished ninth in balloting for the Heisman Trophy. In 1974 and 1975, he had 125 and 132 tackles, respectively. It's no coincidence that OU won national championships both years; in his three years as a starter, OU was 32–1–1. Lee Roy was the first player taken in the 1976 NFL Draft, by the Tampa Bay Buccaneers. Elected to the College Football Hall of Fame in 1988, Selmon became the first OU player enshrined in the Pro Football Hall of Fame, in 1995.

ROD SHOATE
Linebacker, 1972–1974

Former Oklahoma defensive coordinator Larry Lacewell once described Rod Shoate as "the finest defensive player I've ever been around." When you consider the talent Shoate played with—let alone the guys Lacewell has been around—that's pretty high praise. From 1972 to 1974, Shoate tallied 426 tackles while playing, as Barry Switzer said, "like one of those guided missiles." Shoate, a native of Spiro, Oklahoma, regularly tallied double-digit tackle games. He was 31–1–1 as a starter, including a national championship in 1974, and was a consensus All-American in 1973 and 1974. Shoate played in the NFL with New England and Chicago. He died in 1999, at age 46.

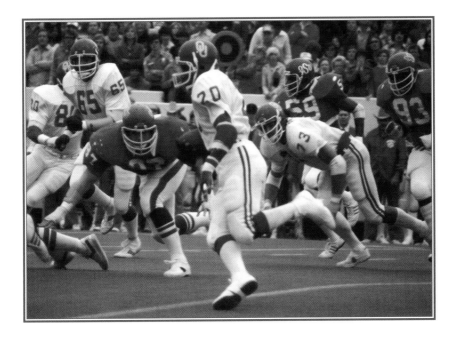

BILLY SIMS
Running Back, 1975–1979

It took a while for Billy Sims to make a mark at OU. When he did, it was indelible. Injuries had beset him as a freshman and sophomore, including a season-ending injury in 1976. In 1978, Sims broke loose for 1,896 yards—an OU single-season record until Adrian Peterson came along in 2004—averaging 7.6 yards per carry and tallying 22 touchdowns. Those stats included three straight 200-yard games, and led Sims to become OU's third Heisman Trophy winner (in 2003, Jason White became the fourth). OU might have been denied the national championship by a loss to Nebraska, in which Sims fumbled deep in Huskers territory in the fourth quarter. The next year, Sims rushed for 1,670 yards and 23 touchdowns, but Southern Cal's Charles White won the award. Sims finished his career with 4,118 yards, the school record. He was the No. 1 overall selection in the 1980 draft and played six years with the Detroit Lions, making the Pro Bowl three times. A knee injury cut short his career. He was inducted into the College Football Hall of Fame in 1995.

CLENDON THOMAS
Halfback, 1955–1957

A consensus All-America selection in 1957, Clendon Thomas was one of the main cogs in the Sooners' NCAA-record 47-game winning streak, including national titles in 1955 and 1956. In 1956, as a junior, Thomas led the nation in scoring. He set the school's three-year scoring record with 37 touchdowns (32 rushing, five receiving). A two-way player—like everyone back then—Thomas returned an interception for a touchdown in the Sooners' 40–0 win over Notre Dame in 1956. Thomas was drafted by Los Angeles in the second round and played four seasons with the Rams. Thomas lives in Oklahoma City and has remained close to the program.

JERRY TUBBS
Center/Linebacker, 1954–1956

Jerry Tubbs's blocking was key to OU's national titles in 1955 and 1956. Although halfbacks Tommy McDonald and Clendon Thomas got the statistics, Tubbs cleared the way. He wasn't any slouch as a linebacker, either. Against Texas in 1955, he intercepted three passes. OU never lost during Tubbs's career. In 1956, Tubbs received the Walter Camp Award as the national Player of the Year, was named lineman of the year by UPI and finished fourth in Heisman Trophy voting (one spot behind teammate Tommy McDonald). Tubbs was the third overall pick in the first round of the NFL draft by the Chicago Cardinals. He later played and coached with the Dallas Cowboys. He was elected to the College Football Hall of Fame in 1996.

BILLY VESSELS
Running Back, 1950–1952

Billy Vessels played in only 24 games as a Sooner, but he was impressive enough to become the school's first Heisman Trophy winner in 1952. From tiny Cleveland, Oklahoma, he was one of Bud Wilkinson's early recruiting finds. Vessels started as a sophomore on the Sooners' 1950 national championship squad. He rushed for 870 yards and 18 touchdowns and threw for three touchdowns. He scored the winning touchdown against Texas on an 11-yard run with less than five minutes left; it was the Longhorns' only loss and propelled OU to the national title. In 1952, when OU finished ranked fourth nationally, Vessels rushed for 1,072 yards and 18 touchdowns (which led the nation). That year he won the Heisman, becoming only the fourth player from west of the Mississippi River to win the award in its then-18-year history. Vessels totaled 2,085 rushing yards and added 327 passing and 391 receiving. He was also a force on kickoff and punt returns. Vessels played two years in the Canadian Football League, spent two years in the army and then played one year in Baltimore before retiring from football. He was elected to the College Football Hall of Fame in 1974 and died in 2001.

JOE WASHINGTON
Running Back, 1972–1975

Texas coach Darrell Royal might have best described the elusive Joe Washington. The Sooners halfback, he said, was like "smoke through a keyhole." OU fans and foes alike remember the dervish in silver shoes who darted this way and that for big plays that helped fuel two national championships. From Port Arthur, Texas, the 5'10" 170-pounder started as a freshman—the first year freshmen were eligible—and joined Greg Pruitt in a backfield for the ages.

Washington was a two-time All-American. He finished third in Heisman voting as a junior in 1974, fifth as a senior in 1975. He ended his career as OU's all-time leading rusher, with 4,071 yards (he now trails Billy Sims). Washington's biggest moment might have come against Missouri in 1975, when on fourth-and-one, he raced 71 yards for a touchdown, then added the two-point conversion, to help the Sooners avoid an upset. They went on to win their second straight national championship. Washington was a first-round selection of the San Diego Chargers and played 10 NFL seasons, mostly with the Washington Redskins. He was elected to the College Football Hall of Fame in 2005.

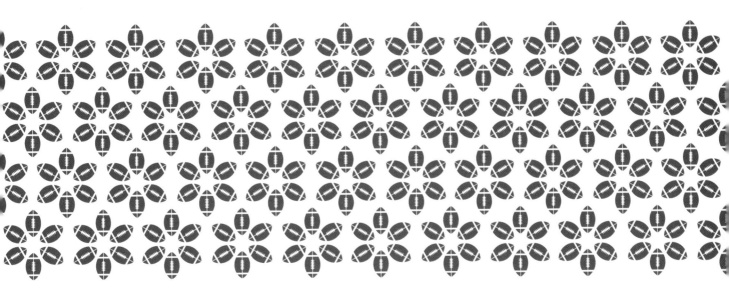

JIM WEATHERALL
Offensive Tackle, 1948–1951

A two-time All-American, Jim Weatherall won the Outland Trophy in 1951 as the nation's top lineman. He was the first Sooner to win a national individual award. Weatherall was large for his day—he stood 6'4" and weighed 230 pounds. Although he was known mostly for his defensive prowess, he was a major contributor on the offensive line as well. He was one of the linchpins on OU's first national title team, in 1950, and his blocking helped OU's 1951 offense rank ninth nationally in rushing offense, seventh in total offense. Weatherall was inducted into the College Football Hall of Fame in 1992.

JASON WHITE
Quarterback, 1999–2004

Favorite son Jason White's success story was embraced by all Oklahoma fans. Born into a blue-collar family and raised in the small town of Tuttle, a farming community about 25 miles west of Norman, White overcame serious adversity to become one of the greatest Sooners ever, going 27–4 as a starter, winning the Heisman Trophy and taking OU to two consecutive BCS national championship games. White brought an unassuming confidence to everything he did. Perhaps his place in Sooner lore was set in 2001, when he came off the bench to help lead OU to a win over Texas. But his legend didn't become national until 2003, when he overcame two blown-out knees to win the Heisman Trophy and lead OU to the brink of the national championship. Once a scrambling, wild colt, White morphed into a precise pocket-passer in 2003—and came from nowhere to win the Heisman Trophy. That year, he threw for 3,846 yards and 40 touchdowns against only 10 interceptions. White was injured when OU lost 21–14 to LSU in the Sugar Bowl, falling just short of the national title. The next year, White finished third in the Heisman balloting, and OU again fell just short of a national title, losing to USC in the Orange Bowl. White's balky knees ended any chance of his playing professional football. He has begun a business career in Oklahoma City.

ROY WILLIAMS
Safety, 1999–2001

One play was all most college football fans remember about Roy Williams. But that signature moment was all they needed to see. Williams's leap-and-crash into Texas quarterback Chris Simms resulted in Teddy Lehman's interception and easy walk-in touchdown that secured a 14–3 win over the Longhorns in 2001. It might have propelled Williams to the Jim Thorpe and Bronko Nagurski awards as the nation's best defensive back and best defensive player, respectively. He also finished seventh in Heisman voting. But that moment illustrated his ability; it didn't define it. From Union City, California, Williams proved the perfect blend of versatility at safety in Bob and Mike Stoops's aggressive defensive schemes. He finished a three-year career with 287 tackles, including 34 for losses (a school record for defensive backs). He had nine interceptions and 44 passes broken up. Williams left school early. He was chosen eighth overall by the Dallas Cowboys and quickly became a Pro Bowl performer. But he remains a frequent visitor to Norman, where his $100,000 donation funded a weight room that carries his name.

Barry Switzer

Bud Wilkins

Bob Stoops

THE COACHES

Oklahoma's football program has been fortunate to feature many great coaches. Bennie Owen took a fledgling program to competitive stature in the early 1900s. Guys like Thomas Stidham and Dewey Luster and Jim Tatum continued the tradition. Others, like Jim MacKenzie, who died after one season, might have become legends. But three names stand above the rest: Bud, Barry and Bob.

Together, the three Bs—Bud Wilkinson, Barry Switzer and Bob Stoops— account for 29 of OU's 39 conference titles, 18 of OU's 24 bowl championships and all seven national championships.

Bud—14 conference championships, six bowl wins, three national championships

Barry—12 conference championships, eight bowl wins, three national championships

Bob—three conference championships, four bowl wins, one national championship

*"**Bud just overwhelmed you** with his personality. As soon as I met him, something clicked that said, 'you'd better go here.' He was just so far ahead of everybody else at that time."* —FORMER ALL-AMERICA HALFBACK TOMMY MCDONALD

—— Bud Wilkinson ——
1947-1963

The author of the NCAA's longest winning streak, Bud Wilkinson built Oklahoma football into a postwar powerhouse and set the stage for more than a half-century in the national spotlight. He arrived in 1947, earned a national championship in 1950 and then—during a 47-game winning streak—grabbed two more in 1955 and 1956.

Heck, Sooner fans will tell you it could have been more. OU was undefeated in 1949 and 1954 but didn't finish atop the national rankings. In the 1950s, OU was an astounding 93–10–2 (.895).

In 17 seasons, Wilkinson's teams compiled a record of 145–29–4, for an unbelievable .826 winning percentage. OU won 14 conference championships, including 12 straight—at one point, the Sooners went unbeaten in 74 conference games (72 wins, two ties). And in an era when going to a bowl was not assured, even if you won the conference, the Sooners won six bowl games.

WILKINSON AT OKLAHOMA

YEAR	RECORD	BOWL
1947*	7–2–1	
1948*	10–1	Sugar
1949*	11–0	Sugar
1950*#	10–1	Sugar
1951**	8–2	
1952**	8–1–1	
1953**	9–1–1	Orange
1954**	10–0	
1955**#	11–0	Orange
1956**#	10–0	
1957**	10–1	Orange
1958***	10–1	
1959***	7–3	
1960	3–6–1	
1961	5–5	
1962***	8–3	Orange
1963	8–2	

* Big 6 champions

** Big 7 champions

*** Big 8 champions

national champions

Wilkinson, a Minnesota native, came to OU as an assistant to Jim Tatum—bringing Wilkinson along had been one of Tatum's prerequisites for taking the job. But when Tatum left for Maryland after one season, the 31-year-old Wilkinson was named head coach. It was a perfect fit.

Wilkinson had an eye for detail, and using the split T formation, he quickly built a monster that still growls more than a half-century after Wilkinson's arrival in Norman.

Wilkinson ran unsuccessfully for the United States Senate in the 1960s, coached the St. Louis Cardinals in 1976–1977 and had success as a sports broadcaster. He died in 1994.

"What Bud built, Barry came in and sustained it and helped it even grow. I think what he accomplished was remarkable." —Bob Stoops

Barry Switzer
1973-1988

No one, it was said, could ever match Bud Wilkinson. But by the time he finished, Barry Switzer had done just that. In 16 seasons, he was 157–29–4. His .837 winning percentage was better than Wilkinson's; like Wilkinson's, Switzer's teams had won three national championships.

Switzer did it with a brash, swashbuckling style. He recruited great players—he was ahead of many of his rivals in integration—and set them free in the wishbone attack. With fleet-footed quarterbacks and halfbacks, the Sooners sped up and down the artificial-turf surfaces installed in the 1970s and 1980s.

The Sooners won national titles in 1974, 1975 and 1985 and just missed several others. They won 12 Big 8 titles. Billy Sims won the Heisman, and a couple of others—Joe Washington and Greg Pruitt—came close. Meanwhile, OU's defenses were filled with big, fast players like Lee Roy Selmon, Rod Shoate, Tony Casillas and Brian Bosworth.

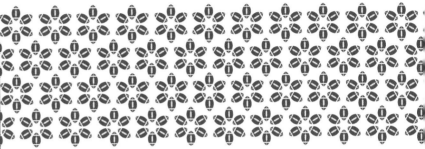

SWITZER AT OKLAHOMA

YEAR	RECORD	BOWL
1973*	10–0–1	
1974*#	11–0	
1975*#	11–1	Orange
1976*	9–2–1	Fiesta
1977*	10–2	Orange
1978*	11–1	Orange
1979*	11–1	Orange
1980*	10–2	Orange
1981	7–4–1	Sun
1982	8–4	Fiesta
1983	8–4	
1984*	9–2–1	Orange
1985*#	11–1	Orange
1986*	11–1	Orange
1987*	11–1	Orange
1988	9–3	Citrus

* Big 8 champions

national champions

Switzer's battles with the straitlaced Tom Osborne, coach of the archrival Nebraska Cornhuskers, were the stuff of legend. It seemed each and every year, the Big 8 title and a berth in the Orange Bowl came down to the teams' late-November battle. More times than not, the Sooners came out on top. But occasionally, it took some of what Switzer termed "Sooner magic"—his way to explain the freak luck that sometimes seemed to accompany OU.

Switzer resigned under pressure amid an NCAA investigation in 1989. He later coached the Dallas Cowboys to a Super Bowl victory. Now retired, he resides in Norman, just blocks from the stadium where he created all that Sooner magic.

*"**He has brought us back** to the pinnacle of college football. Bob is creating his own legend. He inherited a program with great tradition, and he's added to it."* —BARRY SWITZER

—— Bob Stoops ——
1999-present

When he arrived, OU's proud football tradition was in tatters. Where once fans had expected championships, now they just wanted a team that could line up right. But Bob Stoops did not promise he would rebuild the program. He promised to win, and soon.

Consider it done. In Stoops's second season, OU returned to the top of college football, following a 7–5 1999 campaign with a storybook 13–0 season. The Sooners started the season ranked 20th in the AP poll but finished atop 'em all.

And it wasn't a fluke. Since that time, OU has won two more Big 12 championships (for a total of three in six seasons) and played in two more BCS national championship games. They've played in seven bowl games in seven seasons, winning four.

Under Stoops, the wins have again begun sweepin' down the plains—as the Sooners like to adapt the old Rodgers and Hammerstein song, substituting *wins* for *wind*.

In six years, Stoops's record is 75–16, for an .824 winning percentage. After that first

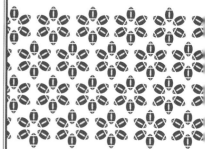

STOOPS AT OKLAHOMA

YEAR	RECORD	BOWL
1999	7–5	Independence
2000*#	13–0	Orange
2001	11–2	Cotton
2002*	12–2	Rose
2003	12–2	Sugar
2004*	12–1	Orange
2005	8–4	Holiday

* Big 12 champions

national champions

season, the record is 68–11 (.861). OU is 5–2 against Texas, including a five-year winning streak (from 2000 to 2004), and has spent 22 weeks ranked at No. 1.

Also included in the growing Stoops legacy: 27 All-Americans and 17 national award winners. Although Stoops's reputation is for fierce, dominating defense, Sooner squads have featured several offensive juggernauts. And that has led to this: Jason White won the Heisman Trophy in 2003. Josh Heupel (2000) and Adrian Peterson (2004)

were Heisman runners-up, and White finished third in the voting in 2004.

A native of Youngstown, Ohio, Stoops started four years as a defensive back at Iowa and was a two-time all–Big Ten selection. He rose through the ranks as an assistant to Bill Snyder at Kansas State, helping that program rise to respectability. Stoops was defensive coordinator at Florida for three years, including 1996, when the Gators won the national championship.

A jubilant group of Sooners brought the 2000 national championship—OU's seventh—home to Norman.

SOONER SUPERLATIVES

In more than 100 years of football, the Oklahoma Sooners have compiled tradition to rival any other school. Seven national championships. Thirty-nine conference titles. Memorable wins. Great plays. Here is a small sample of that record of achievement.

———— The National Championships ————

1950 (AP, UPI)

Coach Bud Wilkinson's fourth Oklahoma team might not have been his best—some claim the 1949 team was better, and perhaps the best-ever Sooner squad. That year OU rolled unbeaten, outscoring opponents 399–88, including a 35–0 win over LSU in the Sugar Bowl, but finished ranked No. 2 (behind Notre Dame).

But the 1950 squad was plenty good. Led by quarterback Claude Arnold and a fast-rising sophomore named Billy Vessels, the Sooners rolled unbeaten through the regular season.

But the season was almost fractured before it had really gotten started. In the second game, OU trailed Texas A&M 28–21 in the fourth quarter. But backed by a raucous home crowd at Memorial Stadium, the Sooners twice drove the length of the field. The winning touchdown came with 69 seconds left: OU won 34–28.

The next week in Dallas, OU again rallied, this time nipping Texas 14–13 on Vessels's 11-yard run with 4:45 left. It was Vessels's second touchdown of the day. Several games later, the Sooners again rallied, this time from a 21–14 halftime deficit against Nebraska. Vessels ran wild, bolting for 208 yards, as the Sooners pulled away, 49–35.

OU's winning streak, which dated to the second game of the 1948 season, was now 31 straight games. But in the Sugar Bowl against Paul "Bear" Bryant's Kentucky squad, the streak was snapped, 13–7.

Although disappointing, the loss didn't matter in terms of the national championship. In those days, when bowls were still viewed as nice bonuses, the final polls were taken after the regular season. OU's 10–0 record then was good enough to keep the Sooners ranked ahead of Army (No. 2 in the AP poll) and Texas (No. 2 in the UPI poll), which had lost only to OU.

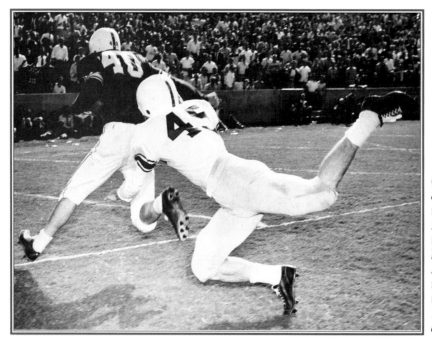

Oklahoma needed every one of the three touchdowns scored by Leon Heath (No. 40) in a tense, come-from-behind win over Texas A&M. The 34–28 victory propelled the Sooners to the 1950 national championship.

1954 Sooners line

The Streak—47 Straight (1953–1957)

Bud Wilkinson's Sooners had earlier tallied a 31-game winning streak. But no one was prepared for what happened from 1953 to 1957. During that golden era, the crimson and cream won 47 straight games.

For years, college football had been an eastern game—or midwestern, because of Notre Dame. But Oklahoma's unprecedented, amazing run established Norman, Oklahoma, as the epicenter of the college football universe.

To put the 47-game streak in perspective, consider that no college team since has gone into a season with a chance to tie the record, let alone break it. (Had USC beaten Texas in the 2006 Rose Bowl, the Trojans would have had a shot—by winning 'em all in the 2006 season.)

What does that mean? Just this: the record, which started with a 19–14 win over Texas and stretched almost five seasons before a stunning

All-conference guard Bill Krisher (shown here stripping an opposing ball carrier) was one of countless contributors to the streak.

7–0 home loss to Notre Dame, will likely never be broken.

Heck, Wilkinson said as much, breaking the stunned silence after the loss to the Fighting Irish: "No major-college football team will ever break this record."

So far, he's been right.

Funny thing. Those Sooners who played during the streak don't remember a whole lot of publicity.

"There was never anything much written about it," said former end Joe Rector. "We weren't really breaking any record. I guess we were setting one."

"It really wasn't on our minds," said quarterback Jimmy Harris, who was 25–0 as a starter

in 1954, 1955 and 1956—and won national titles in the last two seasons.

Now, though, it's something Oklahoma's "Undefeated" will always cherish. Here is a look at the two national championships that came in the midst of the historic streak.

1955 (AP, UPI)

OU's second national title came five years after the first. Again, it might have come earlier. OU entered the 1955 season riding a 19-game winning streak (this one had begun in the third game of the 1953 season). Despite going 10–0 in 1954, the Sooners had been ranked No. 3 in the final polls (behind UCLA and Ohio State, who each grabbed the No. 1 spot in one poll).

In 1955, there was no doubt about the best team in college football. After winning at North Carolina 13–6 in the season opener, the Sooners never again won by fewer than 12 points. OU shut out archrival Texas, 20–0—one of five shutouts tossed by the defense—and then really got rolling.

The average margin of victory: 29 points.

Jimmy Harris, a kid from Terrell, Texas, turned out to be nearly the perfect quarterback to run Bud Wilkinson's split T offense. Tommy McDonald and Clendon Thomas would both make All-American at halfback. And in a precursor to today's no-huddle offenses, the Sooners employed a fast-break offense that wore defenses out in a hurry.

OU averaged 410.7 yards per game. And with the national championship secured—remember, the final polls came out before the bowls—the Sooners had to rally to beat Maryland 20–6 in the Orange Bowl. Trailing 6–0 at halftime, the Sooners went to the fast break and rolled past the Terrapins, who were coached by Jim Tatum—who had coached OU in 1946, bringing a young assistant named Bud Wilkinson along with him, before moving to Maryland.

1956 (AP, UPI)

If 1955 was impressive, 1956 was sheer domination. The Sooners were hardly challenged. They brought back the nucleus from the 1955 team, and just look at the results in another undefeated season and their second straight national championship.

Six shutouts. An average score of 46.6–5.1. That's right—opponents totaled 51 points in 10 games. OU averaged almost 400 rushing yards. A few of the scores: 66–0 over Kansas State, 45–0 over Texas, 40–0 at Notre Dame, 44–0 at Iowa State, 54–6 over Nebraska, and 53–0 over Oklahoma State.

Speaking of 47 straight games, a 40–0 win over Notre Dame marked the end of the

Irish's 47-game streak without being shut out. Eventual Heisman Trophy winner Paul Hornung rushed for seven yards on 13 carries, with three fumbles.

There was one scare. At Boulder, Colorado, OU trailed 19–6 but rallied to win 27–19. Afterward, team members remembered the crowd firing snowballs at the Sooners, to no avail.

Tommy McDonald was named the Maxwell Award winner as college football's top player. Lineman Jerry Tubbs was named the Lineman of the Year and the Walter Camp Player of the Year.

Ending the Streak

Just when Oklahoma appeared invincible, the streak ended. On November 16, 1957, Notre Dame came to Norman and, as a sellout crowd of 63,170 watched in stunned silence, escaped with an upset victory.

"It's just like death," tackle Doyle Jennings said.

OU hadn't been as dominant during the 1957 season, but the Sooners had piled up seven straight wins to run the streak to 47. But on an overcast day, the Fighting Irish stuffed OU's split T offense. And in the fourth quarter, Notre Dame mounted a 20-play, 80-yard drive for the game's only touchdown.

On fourth-and-goal with less than two minutes remaining, halfback Dick Lynch scored on a three-yard run. Then, after OU had driven downfield, Notre Dame quarterback-safety Bob Williams intercepted a pass in the end zone, ending OU's chances of tying the game.

"I thought we'd pull it out," OU senior center Ken Northcutt said after the game.

"We'd been doing it for a long time. You just don't give up."

OU won the last three games of the 1957 season then went 10–1 in 1958. But the streak was over.

"I've had many, many people ask me, 'Oh, did you play in the game that ended the 47-game winning streak?'" said former end Joe Rector. "We were really, really lucky. I don't think that thing will ever be broken."

All good things must come to an end. Despite several chances, OU couldn't get over the hump against Notre Dame in 1957's streak-killing 7–0 loss to the Irish.

1974 NATIONAL CHAMPIONS

The electrifying Joe Washington helped usher in a new era of Sooner dominance.

A New Era: More National Championships

1974 (AP)

He coached three national champions in 16 seasons. But to Barry Switzer, the first might have been the best. Led by speedy halfback Joe Washington and monstrous defenders Lee Roy and Dewey Selmon, the Sooners rolled to an 11–0 record. And despite a television and bowl ban because of NCAA probation, they were awarded the AP's top ranking in the final poll.

It was easy to see why, even if most people never saw them play. OU averaged 507.7 yards per game, leading the nation, and 438.8 rushing yards, also the nation's best. Led by Washington, eight Sooners were named All-Americans.

There were but three close games. OU scored three fourth-quarter touchdowns to beat Baylor early in the season; late in the year, OU overcame a 14–7 third-quarter deficit at Nebraska to win 28–14.

But the most dramatic moments came in Dallas, at the Cotton Bowl, against those hated Longhorns. Texas led 13–7 in the fourth quarter, but a perfectly executed reverse from quarterback Steve Davis to receiver Billy Brooks went for 40 yards and the tying touchdown. Then, the defense stiffened. Jimbo Elrod forced a fumble from Texas freshman fullback Earl Campbell near midfield. Moments later, Tony DiRienzo's 37-yard field goal gave the Sooners a 16–13 win.

The Sooners stayed home for the holidays because of the probation. Because of the sanctions, they were not eligible in the UPI poll; coaches had agreed not to vote for teams on probation. But OU finished No. 1, ahead of USC and Michigan, in the AP poll, claiming its fourth national title.

1975 (AP, UPI)

The 1975 team wasn't nearly as dominant as its immediate predecessor. But the Sooners knew how to win, and with one notable exception, they found ways to do just that.

The wishbone was still a devastatingly effective offense, as run by quarterback Steve Davis and halfback Joe Washington. The Selmon brothers still patrolled the defensive side of the ball, along with several other standouts. But for some reason, the Sooners barely slipped past several opponents.

OU nipped Miami 20–17 in a September game played at the Orange Bowl. The Sooners won one-point decisions over Colorado and Missouri—in both games, the opposing kicker missed an extra point.

And although the Sooners beat Texas 24–17—their fifth straight win over the Longhorns—they needed a trick play to do it. Pinned deep in its own territory, Oklahoma faced third-and-long. But halfback Joe Washington quick-kicked; the 76-yard punt rolled to a stop at the Texas 14 with just more than two minutes left, and the Longhorns had no chance to get downfield for the tying score.

The luck didn't hold, though. Eight turnovers—on eight straight possessions—brought the Sooners crashing down, 23–3, to Kansas in Norman. A 28-game winning streak had ended.

But the "Sooner magic," as Barry Switzer called it, was quickly revived. After blowing a 20-point lead the next week at Missouri, the Sooners got more heroics from Washington. This time, he raced 71 yards for a touchdown on fourth-and-one to pull OU within one, 27–26. Then he ran for the two-point conversion, and OU ran for the exits with that one-point win.

OU faced Michigan in the Orange Bowl, but needed help for any shot at the national title. The Sooners got it when UCLA upset top-ranked Ohio State in the Rose Bowl, which was played earlier in the day. When OU beat Michigan 14–6, it was enough to propel the Sooners to the top of the AP and UPI polls, just ahead of Arizona State and Alabama. In three seasons as a head coach, Switzer had notched two national championships.

Defensive end Jimbo Elrod used quickness, instincts and his wrestling skills to become an All-American. Elrod helped key the Sooner defense during the 1974 and 1975 championship seasons.

Spencer Tillman soars for a score in OU's 1985 season-ender with SMU. The 35–13 win over the Ponies set up a championship showdown with Penn State.

1985 (AP, UPI)

Promising a change from the wishbone to a passing attack, Barry Switzer lured a big, strong-armed Oklahoma kid named Troy Aikman to Norman. Aikman was the starter in 1985—in the wishbone, not a pro passing attack—but when he broke his leg early in the season, it appeared OU had suffered a devastating blow.

Instead, Switzer inserted a freshman speedster named Jamelle Holieway at quarterback—and OU returned to the national championship. Aikman's injury came during a 27–14 loss to Miami at Memorial Stadium.

75

But in the next four games, Holieway ran OU to margins of at least 31 points.

And a dominant defense led by All-Americans Tony Casillas, Brian Bosworth and Kevin Murphy held opponents to just three touchdowns (and 42 points) in the final seven games.

In the annual grudge match with Nebraska, OU rolled 27–7. Tight end Keith Jackson, on his way to a Hall of Fame career, took a reverse 88 yards for a touchdown early in the game, and Holieway scored from 43 and 17 yards out.

In the Orange Bowl, third-ranked OU faced top-ranked Penn State. Meanwhile, in the Sugar Bowl in New Orleans, eighth-ranked Tennessee faced No. 2 Miami—the team that had earlier beaten OU.

Clearly the Sooners not only had to win, but they also needed Tennessee to win. The Vols rolled 35–7. OU won 25–10 and did it with big plays. Holieway connected with Jackson for a 71-yard touchdown and a 10–7 lead. Later, fullback Lydell Carr raced 61 yards for a score.

Thus, the Sooners earned the school's sixth national championship and their first in 10 years.

OU celebrates after beating Texas, 63–14, in 2000.

2000 (AP, ESPN/USA TODAY)

Oklahoma had long been dormant when Bob Stoops arrived. Naysayers suggested the program had slipped too far and that it would never recover. It took Stoops two seasons to bring the Sooners all the way back.

In 2000, the Sooners were ranked No. 19 in the preseason AP poll. It was a nice nod to their modest success of the year before, when they were 7–5. Before the season began? OU dropped to 20th.

From there, though, the Sooners skyrocketed to the top. After winning three non-conference games and beating Kansas in the Big 12 opener, the Sooners faced an October stretch that appeared fearsome. Or maybe not.

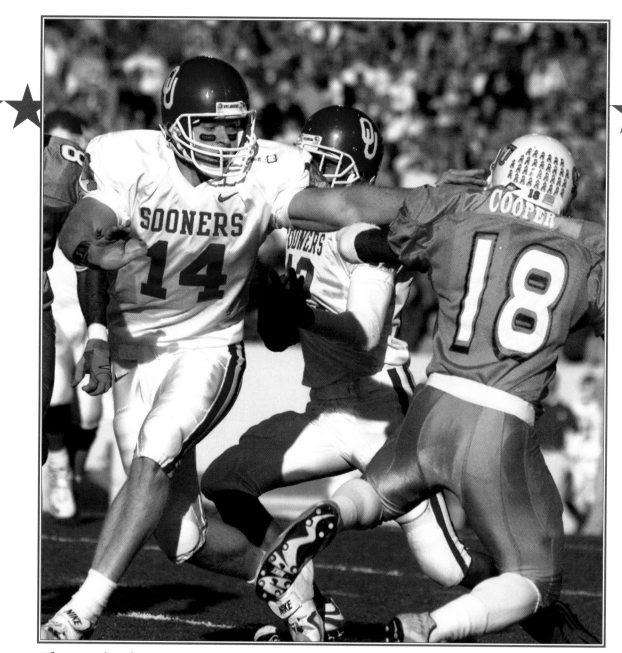

Whatever it takes: OU quarterback Josh Heupel throws a block in Oklahoma's 12–7 Bedlam win on the way to the national title.

Led by Josh Heupel, a cerebral, accurate quarterback who worked the Sooners' spread offense to perfection almost all season, OU stunned Texas, 63–14. The postgame celebration included an impromptu team photograph at midfield with the Cotton Bowl scoreboard in the background.

From there, OU whipped Kansas State on the road. Then, after an off week, OU overcame a 14–0 deficit and rolled top-ranked Nebraska 31–14. When the next polls came out, OU was No. 1 again. And the Sooners never let go of the ranking.

Heupel, a junior-college transfer who had arrived on campus just days after Stoops in December 1998, had morphed into a heady senior whose leadership was the glue that held a group of determined seniors together. Heupel's on-field heroics propelled him from nowhere on the national radar to serious Heisman Trophy contention. He finished runner-up in close voting to Florida State graybeard Chris Weinke—but the quarterbacks would get a chance to settle it on the field.

OU survived late-season scares at Texas A&M and Oklahoma State, beat Kansas State again in the Big 12 championship game and headed for the Orange Bowl, where they were somehow double-digit underdogs to Florida State.

In a defensive struggle, tiny tailback Quentin Griffin's late touchdown run provided the cushion OU needed. Florida State's only score came on a safety after a bad punt snap.

OU's 13–2 win completed a 13–0 season for the school's seventh national championship—and perhaps, given the long decade in decline that preceded it, the sweetest.

CONFERENCE CHAMPIONSHIPS

YEAR	CONFERENCE	OVERALL
1915	3–0 (SWC)	10–0
1918	2–0 (SWC)	6–0
1920	4–0–1 (Mo. Valley)	6–0–1
1938	5–0 (Big 6)	10–1
1943	5–0 (Big 6)	7–2
1944	4–0–1 (Big 6)	6–3–1
1946	4–1 (Big 6)	8–3
1947	4–0–1 (Big 6)	7–2–1
1948	5–0 (Big 7)	10–1
1949	5–0 (Big 7)	11–0
1950	6–0 (Big 7)	10–1
1951	6–0 (Big 7)	8–2
1952	5–0 (Big 7)	8–1–1
1953	6–0 (Big 7)	9–1–1
1954	6–0 (Big 7)	10–0
1955	6–0 (Big 7)	11–0
1956	6–0 (Big 7)	10–0
1957	6–0 (Big 7)	10–1
1958	6–0 (Big 7)	10–1
1959	5–1 (Big 7)	7–3

YEAR	CONFERENCE	OVERALL
1962	7–0 (Big 8)	8–3
1967	7–0 (Big 8)	10–1
1968	6–1 (Big 8)	7–4
1972	6–1 (Big 8)	11–1
1973	7–0 (Big 8)	10–0–1
1974	7–0 (Big 8)	11–0
1975	6–1 (Big 8)	11–1
1976	5–2 (Big 8)	9–2–1
1977	7–0 (Big 8)	10–2
1978	6–1 (Big 8)	11–1
1979	7–0 (Big 8)	11–1
1980	7–0 (Big 8)	10–2
1984	6–1 (Big 8)	9–2–1
1985	7–0 (Big 8)	11–1
1986	7–0 (Big 8)	11–1
1987	7–0 (Big 8)	11–1
2000	8–0 (Big 12)	13–0
2002	6–2 (Big 12)	12–2
2004	8–0 (Big 12)	12–1

—— The Greatest Games ——

OKLAHOMA 34, TEXAS A&M 28
OCTOBER 7, 1950

Trailing 28–21 late in the fourth quarter, it appeared OU's unbeaten season was about to be blemished. Billy Vessels scored on a pass from Claude Arnold, but kicker Jim Weatherall missed the extra point, leaving OU behind by a point with 3:36 left. When OU got the ball back with 1:46 left, Arnold led the Sooners 69 yards, completing four of five passes. Fullback Leon Heath scored on a four-yard run with 37 seconds left to give OU the win.

NOTRE DAME 7, OKLAHOMA 0
NOVEMBER 16, 1957

OU's NCAA-record 47-game winning streak ended on an overcast day at Owen Field. Notre Dame stopped the Sooners' vaunted split T offense, but the Irish couldn't move, either. Through three quarters, there was no score.

But on fourth-and-goal from the 3 with 3:50 left, Notre Dame halfback Dick Lynch found the end zone. OU moved downfield in desperation, but Notre Dame's Bob Williams intercepted a pass in the end zone. Seconds later, the streak was finished.

OKLAHOMA 17, USC 12
SEPTEMBER 28, 1963

As a sun-baked crowd watched at the Los Angeles Coliseum in 100-degree heat, the Sooners put together a road upset over the defending national champion Trojans. Realizing his team was outmanned, coach Bud Wilkinson chose to grind it out. OU ran on 77 of 89 plays. The strategy worked. Joe Don Looney gave OU the first-quarter lead on a 19-yard run, and the Sooners got 10 more points in the third quarter to stretch the lead to 11—enough to hold off USC.

Oklahoma coach Chuck Fairbanks (right) jokes with Nebraska coach Bob Devaney prior to 1971's Game of the Century.

NEBRASKA 35, OKLAHOMA 31
NOVEMBER 25, 1971

They still call it the "Game of the Century," and with good reason. Although it didn't turn out the way Sooner fans had hoped, it is remembered as a classic battle of intensity between rivals. No. 1 Nebraska came to Norman to play No. 2 OU. President Nixon came to town, too. And a nationwide audience watched on ABC. At stake: the Big 8 title and a berth in the Orange Bowl—where Alabama and the national championship awaited. Both teams played very well.

Nebraska's future Heisman winner Johnny Rodgers broke a 72-yard punt return that gave Nebraska the early lead. And although OU came back from 11-point deficits twice—Jack Mildren's pass to split end Jon Harrison pushed the Sooners up 31–28 with 7:10 left—the Huskers came out on top. Jeff Kinney rushed for 50 of 74 yards on a 12-play drive that broke Sooners' hearts. Kinney's one-yard touchdown run with 1:38 left sent the Huskers on to what would become their second straight national title.

OKLAHOMA 28, MISSOURI 27
NOVEMBER 15, 1975

Just a week earlier, a 28-game winning streak had ended with a devastating 23–3 home loss to Kansas. And at Columbia, Missouri, the Sooners appeared to be on the verge of starting a losing streak. OU had blown a 20–0 lead and trailed 27–20 in the fourth quarter. But Joe Washington took over. On fourth-and-one from Oklahoma's own 29, Barry Switzer called for the ball to be given to Washington, hoping to extend the drive. Washington did much more than that, bolting 71 yards for a touchdown with 4:20 left. Then he ran the same play for the two-point conversion that gave the Sooners a dramatic victory.

OKLAHOMA 29, OHIO STATE 28
SEPTEMBER 24, 1977

They simply call it "the Kick." Uwe von Schamann booted his way into Sooner lore with one incredible moment that ended an incredible matchup between national power-houses. As 88,119 watched at Ohio Stadium, OU grabbed a 20–0 lead, only to watch the Buckeyes come roaring back for 28 straight points. OU scored on Elvis Peacock's one-yard run with 1:29 left, but the two-point conversion failed, and it appeared Ohio State would prevail. But OU's Mike Babb recovered von Schamann's onside kick. Dean Blevins, subbing for an injured Thomas Lott, tossed a pass to the Ohio State 23 with three seconds left. OU called timeout to allow von Schamann to set up, and then the Buckeyes called timeout to try to ice him. It didn't work. Ohio State fans chanted, "Block that kick! Block that kick!" And von Schamann taunted them, waving his arms like a music conductor.

His 40-yard field goal sailed true; the Horseshoe was silent—and OU had an incredible victory.

Uwe von Schamann and Bud Herbert jump for joy after von Schamann's field goal beats Ohio State 29–28 in the final seconds of the now-legendary game played in 1977.

Barry Switzer gets a ride from jubilant players following their win over Penn State in the 1986 Orange Bowl in Miami, Florida.

OKLAHOMA 21, NEBRASKA 17
NOVEMBER 22, 1980

As usual, Oklahoma and Nebraska met with the Big 8 title on the line. The Huskers led late, and the home crowd in Lincoln had tossed oranges onto the field—the traditional action of both fan bases to celebrate securing an Orange Bowl berth. Except the Huskers hadn't quite done it. OU rolled 80 yards in eight plays—the big play was Buster Rhymes's 43-yard run on the option, which moved OU to the 14. Five plays later, Rhymes's dive over the pile for a touchdown with less than a minute left gave the ninth-ranked Sooners a mild upset over No. 4–ranked Nebraska.

OKLAHOMA 13,
OKLAHOMA STATE 0
NOVEMBER 30, 1985

In sub-zero temperatures, the Sooners battled their in-state rivals. Lewis Field in Stillwater was covered with ice and snow. Neither team could move without slipping and sliding. But freshman quarterback Jamelle Holieway threw for 54 yards and ran for 51 more—good numbers considering the conditions. Tim Lashar hit two field goals, and Spencer Tillman ran three yards for a score. OSU, meanwhile, managed just 131 total yards, most by future NFL star Thurman Thomas.

OKLAHOMA 25, PENN STATE 10
JANUARY 1, 1986
ORANGE BOWL

After getting help from Tennessee, which upset No. 2 Miami in the Sugar Bowl, OU needed only to beat No. 1 Penn State to secure the national championship. No problem. Tim Lashar hit four field goals—an Orange Bowl record—and Keith Jackson and Lydell Carr supplied big plays as the Sooners won 25–10. Penn State had grabbed an early 7–0 lead, but Lashar's field goal was followed by Jackson's 71-yard catch-and-run from Jamelle Holieway, giving OU the lead. Later Carr put the game away with a 61-yard romp for a score.

OKLAHOMA 17, NEBRASKA 7
NOVEMBER 21, 1987

Another year, another showdown with Nebraska. They called this one "Game of the Century II." No. 1 Nebraska had a high-powered offense but was shut down by the Sooners. Nebraska averaged 524 yards per game but managed only 235 against an inspired OU defense. Rickey Dixon had two interceptions, including one that set up OU's first touchdown. Nebraska crossed midfield only three times. Meanwhile, freshman quarterback Charles Thompson, starting because of an injury to Jamelle Holieway, was one of three OU players with more than 100 yards. Patrick Collins's 65-yard TD run in the third quarter gave OU the lead, and R.D. Lashar's field goal put it out of reach.

OKLAHOMA 38, TEXAS 17
OCTOBER 9, 1993

The Sooners had lost four straight to their hated rivals, and with starting quarterback Cale Gundy hampered by a strained hip muscle, the team didn't appear to have much of a chance. Instead, OU never trailed. Gundy ran for three touchdowns, including an 18-yarder. The Sooners built a 31–10 lead and dominated the Longhorns.

OKLAHOMA 30, TEXAS 27
OCTOBER 12, 1996

OU football was in dire straits. By the time the Sooners arrived in Dallas, any thoughts of a winning season were gone; folks just hoped for a win sometime during the season. No one expected it to come against Texas, but led by James Allen's 210 yards of total offense (159 yards rushing), the Sooners overcame an early 10–0 deficit, rallied for 11 points in the fourth quarter to force overtime and then won on Allen's two-yard run.

The gathering crowd on the field attempts to pull down a goal post after OU defeats Nebraska, 31–14, on October 28, 2000.

OKLAHOMA 31, NEBRASKA 14
OCTOBER 28, 2000

OU had routed Texas, 63–14. The Sooners had beaten Kansas State, 41–31. And if any questions about OU's sudden resurgence lingered, they were answered on one glorious Saturday. Top-ranked Nebraska came to Owen Field to face the third-ranked Sooners; after a decade in decline, it was a matchup worthy of the rivalry. After spotting the Huskers a 14–0 first-quarter lead on drives of 76 and 91 yards—the crowd was stunned, but the Sooners weren't— OU roared back, dominating the last three quarters to beat Nebraska for the first time since 1990. Nebraska had 167 yards and those two touchdowns on its first 11 plays, but the team managed only 161 yards in its final 59 plays. Meanwhile, OU's offense got untracked, exploding for 24 second-quarter points, including Josh Heupel's 34-yard TD connection with Curtis Fagan. Heupel finished with 300 yards on 20-of-34 passing. Fittingly, Derrick Strait's 32-yard interception return for a touchdown was the only score of the second half. OU moved to No. 1 in the polls and never looked back.

Oklahoma coach Bob Stoops (left) celebrates with players J.T. Thatcher (No. 15) and Ontei Jones (No. 11) as they pose with the trophy after beating Florida State 13–2 in the 2001 Orange Bowl. Looking on at right is Orange Bowl president Sherrill Hudson.

OKLAHOMA 13, FLORIDA STATE 2
JANUARY 3, 2001
ORANGE BOWL

Defense wins championships. It's a cliché, sure. But it was never truer than on this night, when the Sooners shut down the Seminoles' high-octane offense. Florida State never sniffed the end zone, managing only 27 rushing yards; the Seminoles' only score came when OU's misfired deep snap resulted in a safety. OU's offense, meanwhile, was efficient, holding the ball for more than 36 minutes. Tim Duncan hit two field goals, and in the fourth quarter, Quentin Griffin secured victory with his twisting, bouncing 10-yard touchdown run. Josh Heupel finished as runner-up to FSU's Chris Weinke in the Heisman voting, and Weinke threw for 274 yards (on 25-of-51 passing, with two interceptions). But Heupel put together a steady 214-yard performance (25-of-39). And by the end of the game, OU fans were serenading the teams with: "Heupel Heisman! Heupel Heisman!" No one argued. And the more important trophy, the BCS's crystal football, was hoisted high by a host of Sooners.

OKLAHOMA 14, TEXAS 3
OCTOBER 6, 2001

A dominant Sooner defense—perhaps the best of the Bob Stoops era—dehorned Texas in a thriller at the Cotton Bowl. And one spectacular play defined the game. With starting quarterback Nate Hybl injured, a youngster named Jason White came in and led the Sooners to a touchdown. But OU's lead was a perilous 7–3 late in the fourth quarter when Texas got the ball deep in its own territory. Chris Simms dropped back to pass—and OU super safety Roy Williams leaped over a would-be blocker and crashed into Simms, knocking the football toward the line of scrimmage. There, linebacker Teddy Lehman grabbed it and sauntered easily into the end zone. Game over. And Williams's career defined.

OKLAHOMA 20, ALABAMA 13
SEPTEMBER 6, 2003

A year earlier, OU had barely escaped Alabama at Owen Field. And on a muggy night in the Deep South, it appeared the Crimson Tide might have laid an upset trap on the No. 1–ranked Sooners. But two quick strikes and a trick play helped OU win. Jason White tossed long touchdown passes to Mark Clayton and Brandon Jones. But the pass to Jones came only after Bob Stoops reached deep into his bag of tricks. OU led 13–10 in the third quarter when, facing fourth-and-10 from his own 31, Stoops gambled. Punter Blake Ferguson didn't kick; he tossed a short pass to reserve defensive back Michael Thompson, who bobbled the ball and then raced 22 yards for a first down. On the next play, White hit Jones for 47 yards and a touchdown. And OU held the ball for more than nine minutes in the fourth quarter to extinguish Alabama's hope.

Teddy Lehman is tackled after an interception in the third quarter, October 12, 2002.

THE RIVALRIES

Oklahoma has long been a part of three great rivalries. The annual battles with Texas take on biblical proportions, and have only grown since the schools became conference opponents. It seemed OU-Nebraska determined the Big 8 championship almost every year. And although OU owns a lopsided series advantage over Oklahoma State, the annual tilt with the Cowboys often lives up to its name: Bedlam.

The Red River Shootout

Oil wells have been known to change hands as a result of wagers on the outcome. The game is played every year at a neutral site—Dallas, Texas. Oil country. And the graduates and devotees of both schools, Oklahoma and Texas, raise the stakes off the field almost as high as those riding on the game itself.

The backdrop is the Texas State Fair. Cotton Bowl Stadium. Second weekend of October. Fan entourages equally divided between those arrayed in crimson and those in burnt orange, the line of demarcation drawn sharply down the 50-yard line. The Red River Shootout.

"It's a great week. It doesn't get any better," OU coach Bob Stoops said. "Our players really enjoy and love this week. We do as coaches. You love the challenge of it, the competition of it and the excitement of going into their state fair and going into the Cotton Bowl and playing and competing with Texas.

"It's the best. Pulling into the stadium, getting dressed, it's hard to wait for kickoff. It's exciting. It brings out the best in you and gets the hair up on the back of your neck. It's just what you want."

A major bowl atmosphere surrounds this event when two of the most tradition-gorged programs in college football battle it out. Between the two, they have won 11 national championships.

But it wasn't always so. The two schools first met on the gridiron in 1900, seven years before Oklahoma was admitted to the union as a state. Texas won that first contest 28–2, and the next four after that, including two in 1901. Texas, then known as the Steers, treated the Oklahoma game as a practice workout. But OU's first win came in 1905, 2–0 on a safety. It

was just a matter of time before Oklahoma became competitive on a national level.

From 2000 to 2004, OU won five straight over the Longhorns. And each year, the game served as a springboard for the Sooners' run at a national title.

Until the inception of the Big 12 in 1996, Oklahoma-Texas had been a nonconference game since OU jumped from the Southwest Conference to the Big 6 (later to become the Big 8) in 1920. The game moved permanently to the Texas State Fair in 1929 and from the outset was the main event. Texas won that first meeting in Dallas 21–0, with the Longhorns in the midst of a six-game winning streak over the Sooners.

Although the game has long been the biggest one on the Sooners' schedule, it took on more importance when the schools became rivals for the Big 12 South title. It used to be that a loss didn't cripple the teams' conference title hopes. OU could still go on to earn an Orange Bowl berth, Texas the Cotton Bowl

In two consecutive Red River contests—a 14–3 defensive struggle in 2001 and a 35–24 shootout in 2002—Teddy Lehman came up with game-changing interceptions.

Rufus Alexander forces a Vince Young fumble in Oklahoma's 12–0 whitewash of Texas in 2004, the Sooners' fifth consecutive win in the series.

berth (as SWC champion). But now the game almost always decides the Big 12 South race—and that usually means it decides the Big 12 title.

National title hopes are extended—or dashed. The rivalry is bigger than ever.

"Our games were important," former OU coach Barry Switzer said. "This game has more weight. [Before] you could probably lose or tie and still have a chance to win the national championship. It was an intersectional game. Now it's much more than intersectional.

"The weight of this is much greater."

Nine times both teams have been ranked in the top five. Of those games, OU has won five, Texas has won three, and there's been a tie—that infamous game in 1984. Three times, the winner of those top-five matchups went on

to claim the national championship (Texas 1963, OU 1974 and 1975).

"I think this game will be this way from now on," Texas coach Mack Brown said. "It's two programs that should be good each year."

Regardless of whether the programs have been good, the rivalry has been great. In 1958, Texas upended the No. 2–ranked Sooners 15–14 on Bobby Lackey's seven-yard touchdown pass to Bob Bryant with 3:10 remaining. That game ended a six-game winning streak by the Sooners over the 'Horns—and started an eight-game winning streak by the 'Horns over the Sooners. Both streaks are the longest for the respective programs.

There have been plenty of other classics, too. Here are a few.

Red River Classics

Score: Oklahoma 24, Texas 17; Date: October 11, 1975

En route to their second straight national championship, the Sooners edged Texas on Horace Ivory's 33-yard touchdown run with 5:31 remaining. The game had been tied 17–17 until the Sooners went 79 yards in seven plays, with Ivory getting most of the yards on one winning romp.

Ivory, by the way, had moved from halfback to fullback because of an injury to starter Jim Littrell. That's why he was in position to score the TD.

But that wasn't the play of the game. It came a little later, and it was produced by Sooner All-America tailback Joe Washington. But it wasn't a run. It was a quick kick. From the shadows of the OU goal line, Washington booted a 76-yarder, reversing the field. Texas couldn't move the ball, and OU won.

Score: OU 15, Texas 15; Date: October 13, 1984

Texas was ranked No. 1, OU No. 2. Neither won. In one of the more controversial endings, Texas forged a tie as time expired—but only after Sooner Keith Stanberry's interception in the end zone was ruled incomplete by an official who said he was out of bounds. Replays clearly showed he was in-bounds.

Jeff Ward's 32-yard field goal tied it on the next play, as the final horn sounded.

The Sooners also remember a fumble that was recovered by OU in the late minutes, only to have the Texas player ruled down; the ball remained with Texas.

Score: OU 30, Texas 27; Date: October 12, 1996

The Sooners were a desperate 0–4 entering the game and were riding a seven-game losing streak—the longest in school history. Texas would go on to win the Big 12 championship. But on this day, the underdog Sooners upset the Longhorns.

OU rallied from an 11-point deficit to tie in the last seven minutes; one of the scores came on Jarrail Jackson's 51-yard punt return for a TD with 6:44 left. And in overtime, James Allen bolted two yards for the winning touchdown—he accounted for all of the Sooners' overtime yards.

Score: OU 14, Texas 13; Date: October 14, 1950

En route to its first national title, OU handed Texas its only loss when Billy Vessels—a sophomore who would win the Heisman Trophy two years later—ran for two touchdowns. Vessels's 11-yard run with 3:46 left gave OU the win. But the TD came after OU's Dean Smith and Frankie Anderson had tackled Texas punter Bill Porter, who could not handle a low snap, at the Texas 11.

Score: OU 14, Texas 3; Date: October 6, 2001

A backup quarterback named Jason White filled in for injured starter Nate Hybl and led OU to its only offensive touchdown—the beginning of a legendary career. But it was OU's defense, and a safety named Roy Williams, that won the game.

Texas struggled against the Sooners' defense all day. And late in the game, Williams's leaping collision with quarterback Chris Simms forced a fluttering loose ball that linebacker Teddy Lehman intercepted near the goal line. Touchdown. Game over.

And that's how it has gone. Win or lose, it's the game every Oklahoma fan has circled on the calendar every year.

"This game is what college football is all about," former tight end Trent Smith said.

Billy Sims and the Sooners trounced Nebraska 38-7 in 1977, OU's sixth straight win in the series.

—— Nebraska ——

If it's not OU-Texas, then OU-Nebraska has been what college football is all about.

The Game of the Century. Game of the Century II. Swashbuckling Barry Switzer versus straitlaced Tom Osborne. Thanksgiving. Crimson versus fire-engine red.

And, to Huskers fans' chagrin: Sooner magic.

Unlike OU's other rivalries, OU-Nebraska had not been about bad blood. There was something more like grudging respect. The game was about championships.

The clash between the different shades of red has been one of the most eagerly anticipated matchups of the year. Often it decided the Big 8 championship and the coveted Orange Bowl berth. Not a few times, national championship hopes were on the line.

"There's a foggy mystique about this whole rivalry," former Nebraska tailback Dan Alexander said.

The rivalry really started with Bob Devaney, Osborne's legendary predecessor. He arrived in Lincoln, Nebraska, in 1962. Five times in the next 25 years, the winner of OU-Nebraska went on to win the national championship. Six more times, the winner played for the national title in a bowl game.

And the games were often good. Twelve times from 1970 to 1988, the game was decided by a touchdown or less. Often, OU came out on top in those close ones, aided by Sooner magic. In 1976, 1980 and 1986, the Sooners pulled out nearly miraculous wins.

Of course, Nebraska won the most famous close one, the 1971 Game of the Century, which

GAME DAY: OKLAHOMA FOOTBALL

was highlighted by Johnny Rodgers's spectacular punt return for a touchdown—and just maybe, an uncalled clipping penalty.

"Oklahoma certainly was the most memorable game of the year," Osborne said years after his retirement from coaching—and during his tenure as a congressman. "It was usually the last game of the year. ... As the series wore on, it seemed like it didn't make much difference what you did your previous 10 games; if you didn't win that one, you didn't really have a good year."

Said OU defensive line coach Jackie Shipp, who played against the Huskers in the 1980s: "You always knew you were going to be in for a very physical game when you played Nebraska. It was a game where the fans always got their money's worth."

OU's decline in the 1990s dampened the rivalry for a while. Nebraska won seven straight. And then the formation of the Big 12 further slowed the rivalry. OU and Nebraska no longer play every year. Because of the split-division format, the teams play two years and then take two years off.

But in 2000 and 2001, the magic was back. OU's 31–14 win in 2000—the Sooners spotted the No. 1–ranked Huskers two touchdowns on their first two possessions, then dominated—sent the Sooners hurtling toward their seventh national championship.

A year later in Lincoln, the Huskers snapped No. 1–ranked OU's 20-game winning streak.

The rivalry's fire was stoked in 2004. OU beat Nebraska handily, 30–3. But during pregame warm-ups, a Nebraska player was involved in an altercation with one of Oklahoma's Ruf-Neks, the unofficial spirit group. The Ruf-Nek was carried off the field on a stretcher after a collision. The Nebraska player was later tried and acquitted of assault charges.

And that was just part of the night's extracurricular activity. As he came off the field after the loss, frustrated first-year Nebraska coach Bill Callahan yelled "F*ck*ng hillbillies!" toward the OU fans.

Never mind that Callahan apparently hadn't studied the geography of Norman. The comment quickly inflamed tensions, at least for a little while.

102

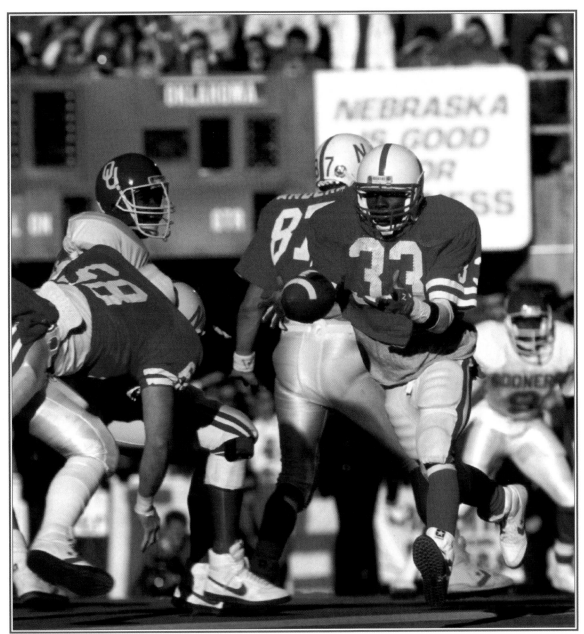

For years, Oklahoma-Nebraska was the game in the Big 8.

OU-Nebraska Classics

Score: Oklahoma 20, Nebraska 17;
Date: November 26, 1976

This is what they call Sooner magic. Unbelievable big plays. Fortuitous bounces. Whatever. In 1976, OU's touchdown with 38 seconds left gave the Sooners the win. The score came after quarterback Dean Blevins passed to Steve Rhodes—who promptly pitched to Elvis Peacock, who rambled 32 yards to keep the drive going.

Score: Nebraska 17, Oklahoma 14;
Date: November 11, 1978

The top-ranked Sooners fumbled away a chance at another national championship—literally. Heisman winner Billy Sims fumbled at the Nebraska 3 with three minutes left. "I felt nauseated for Billy, for Oklahoma, for me," Barry Switzer remembered. "Especially since Billy made a great run to get to the 3."

OU laughed last, though. Although Nebraska won the Big 8 and the automatic Orange Bowl berth, the bowl committee invited OU as the at-large team. The Sooners exacted revenge with a 31–24 victory.

Score: Nebraska 28, Oklahoma 21;
Date: November 26, 1983

Nebraska quarterback Turner Gill keyed a late drive for the winning touchdown with a 40-yard run. But Nebraska's defense secured victory. OU's Danny Bradley threw into the end zone on the final play, but Huskers cornerback Neil Harris deflected the pass.

Score: Oklahoma 20, Nebraska 17;

Date: November 22, 1986

After a 94-yard drive for the tying touchdown, which came with 1:22 left, the Sooners got the ball back and went 51 yards to set up Tim Lashar's 31-yard, game-winning field goal with six seconds left. The field goal came after All-America tight end Keith Jackson's one-handed grab of a tough pass from Jamelle Holieway.

Score: Nebraska 20, Oklahoma 10;

Date: October 27, 2001

Oklahoma entered Memorial Stadium riding a 20-game winning streak and ranked No. 1. The Huskers won when quarterback Eric Crouch, who would go on to win the Heisman Trophy, grabbed a quarterback throwback pass and outraced OU defenders into the end zone. Ironically, OU had earlier tried a similar play and it was similarly wide-open. But freshman receiver Mark Clayton's pass to quarterback Nate Hybl was low; Hybl slipped to the ground trying to corral it, and the Huskers exhaled.

The game was also marred by Jason White's torn ACL—the first of two season-ending knee injuries he would suffer before returning to win the Heisman in 2003.

——— Bedlam ———

The rivalry between Oklahoma and Oklahoma State has long been a one-sided affair in football. In an even 100 games, OU leads the all-time series 77–16–7.

OU fans will tell you Texas and Nebraska are bigger rivalries.

But don't misunderstand.

This rivalry might be the most heated of 'em all.

It's like this: Lose to Nebraska, Sooner fans go on with life. Lose to Texas, and Sooner fans growl and grouse, and go on with life.

Lose to OSU, and Sooner fans hear it at work, on the golf course, in the grocery store. From friends, neighbors—even family. So when OSU wins, it makes for a long, long year.

So forget the overall history—OU won the first 11 games and has five winning streaks of at least seven straight; the Sooners won 19 straight and 15 straight at different times.

Go instead to recent history. In the last 11 years, OU has won six, OSU five.

And none was more stunning than the 16–13 loss in 2001. That one left former tight end Trent Smith stewing for the next 365 days.

"If OU wins the game, you don't really hear much about it outside the Sunday paper," Smith said. "If OSU wins, it's Christmas all year for 'em. A freakin' orange Christmas.

"I don't like it when OSU gets to have Christmas all year and I don't."

That 16–13 loss was the biggest upset in OU football history—and was celebrated by OSU fans as one of their biggest wins. The Cowboys entered the game 3–7, 27-point underdogs. OU, meanwhile, still had hopes of defending its 2000 national championship.

Despite a loss to Nebraska a few weeks earlier, OU was in position to win the Big 12 South and perhaps to get a shot at the Rose Bowl and the national championship.

Instead, the Sooners were undone by a sluggish offense and by one OSU drive. OSU had mustered nothing against a fierce OU defense until the final minutes.

Freshman quarterback Josh Fields completed a long pass to T.D. Bryant—just in front of Sooner safety Roy Williams. A moment later, Fields's lob to the front corner of the end zone was hauled in by Rashaun Woods, and the Cowboys celebrated on Owen Field.

Maybe it shouldn't have been so surprising. A year earlier, in 2000, OU's national championship run barely survived a trip to Stillwater. The Sooners won 12–7.

Which brings us back to Trent Smith's orange Christmas; he made the comment in the week leading up to the 2002 game, still smarting from that 2001 loss. And in 2002, OSU beat OU again.

But the Sooners have since won three straight, including a couple of blowouts. They exacted revenge—and in a big way—in 2003, blowing out the Cowboys 52–9 in Norman.

"Probably my favorite win," said former defensive tackle Dusty Dvoracek, who played in a bunch of wins during his career. "Best feeling I've ever had winning a football game."

But in 2004, the Sooners escaped Stillwater with a 38–35 victory when a field goal sailed awry in the final seconds.

By the way, the taunting goes both ways. Riding that three-game streak, OU fans might be the ones who are tough for OSU fans to live with. Ask a Sooner, and he'll tell you that's the natural order of things.

"The thing that stands out in my mind," former OU receiver Curtis Fagan once said, "is this state is a Sooner State."

The Sooners know that to keep it that way they must prevail in Bedlam. Most often, they do.

"It's a big-time deal," Dvoracek said. "I think OU's dominated in the past, but here lately, OSU's playing really good football. They've got our number more than we've got theirs. It's a huge game for us. Now I really appreciate this rivalry.

"It's Bedlam. It's a huge game for us. It's the in-state rival. ... It's huge for our fans. Whoever wins or loses, they're going to hear about it all year. That's all they're going to talk about."

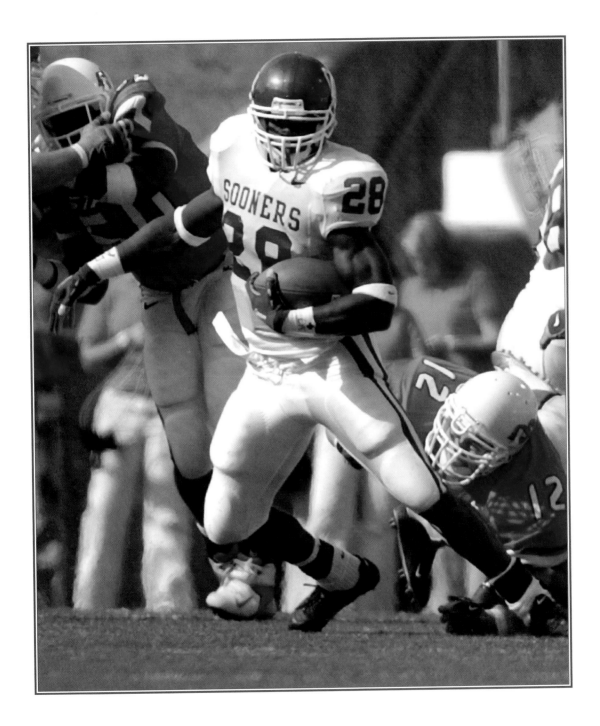

How's this for domination: in two games against Oklahoma State, Adrian Peterson has rushed for 486 yards and four touchdowns.

Bedlam Classics

Score: Oklahoma 38, OSU 35; Date: October 30, 2004

The Sooners were on their way to another Big 12 championship and a shot at the national title, but the Cowboys lay in wait in Stillwater. OU struggled against OSU's deep passing attack. Late in the game, the Cowboys moved downfield with a chance to tie or win. Jason Ricks lined up for a 49-yard field goal with 15 seconds remaining, but the kick sailed wide left.

Score: Oklahoma 31, OSU 28; Date: November 5, 1988

The teams staged a classic in Stillwater. OU led by three points late, but the Cowboys were driving. A taunting penalty forced OSU into fourth-and-16 with 56 seconds left. But quarterback Mike Gundy dropped back and found an open receiver, Brent Parker, in the end zone. Parker dropped the football. OU won.

Score: Oklahoma 28, OSU 27; Date: November 29, 1969

With 1:15 left, OSU scored to pull within a point. Eschewing the tie, the Cowboys went for the two-point conversion. And OU's Albert Qualls sacked Cowboys quarterback Bob Cutberth, ending the threat.

Score: Oklahoma 21, OSU 20; Date: October 15, 1983

OSU rolled early and held a 20–3 lead in the fourth quarter. But Sooner magic took hold. OU scored 17 points in the last 10 minutes. Tim Lashar nailed a 46-yard field goal to give the Sooners the win.

Bob Stoops

TALKIN' OKLAHOMA FOOTBALL

We thought we'd go straight to the source and let some of Oklahoma's greatest legends—and others with a unique perspective—share their thoughts about Sooner football. They put it much better than we could.

"Our players recognize the history of Oklahoma is about winning championships. We already had six national championships. Now, we have seven. You can't say, 'Well that was then, this is now.' This is Oklahoma football." —OKLAHOMA COACH BOB STOOPS AFTER BEATING FLORIDA STATE IN THE ORANGE BOWL TO WIN THE 2000 NATIONAL CHAMPIONSHIP

"I think now it's easy to say that Oklahoma is officially back!" —STOOPS, HOLDING THE CRYSTAL FOOTBALL IN THE MOMENTS AFTER OU WON THE 2000 NATIONAL CHAMPIONSHIP

"When Switzer walks into your home, you relax." —FORMER OU ALL-AMERICA TIGHT END KEITH JACKSON, DESCRIBING HOW BARRY SWITZER LURED HIM FROM LITTLE ROCK TO NORMAN

"Football, in its purest form, remains a physical fight. As in any fight, if you don't want to fight, it's impossible to win." —BUD WILKINSON ON HIS PHILOSOPHY OF SPORT

"There was never a doubt we were not gonna whip anybody. We were bigger, stronger and in better shape. Even when time ran out on Notre Dame it was just time ran out before we beat 'em. We had more will to win than most everyone." —CLENDON THOMAS, EXPLAINING THE SOONERS' CONFIDENCE DURING THE 47-GAME WINNING STREAK

"Bud Wilkinson created the monster in the 1950s, and since that time we've been trying to feed it." —FORMER OU QUARTERBACK AND U.S. REPRESENTATIVE J.C. WATTS

"Coach Wilkinson was a very innovative, dominant coach. Switzer came in and recruited bigger and better players than anybody else around. What you've got with Bob [Stoops] is not only a highly intelligent person, but he and his coaches are also very good recruiters." —JIMMY HARRIS, WHO QUARTERBACKED OU TO NATIONAL CHAMPIONSHIPS IN 1955 AND 1956 AND FINISHED HIS CAREER 25–0 AS A STARTER

"He gets the ball and all of a sudden, he's just fighting. Some guys get tired. Some guys can't play every snap. They've got to come out and get their wind. But he's just a machine. He goes and goes and goes. He's never tired. He's a great athlete, but he's got a motor, too."* —BOB STOOPS, DESCRIBING FORMER OU ALL-AMERICA RECEIVER MARK CLAYTON*

"We came from nowhere to national champions in two years. That's pretty special."* —BOB STOOPS AFTER WINNING THE 2000 NATIONAL TITLE*

Leon Cross

"Everybody will tell you, *Lee Roy was unreal. I never saw him blocked to the ground."* —OU HALFBACK JOE WASHINGTON, REFERRING TO THE PLAYER MANY CONSIDER THE BEST IN SCHOOL HISTORY AT ANY POSITION

"I came to Oklahoma *because of the tradition, the coaches, the players. I just hope I added to it."* —LEON CROSS, WHO WAS AN ALL-AMERICA GUARD-LINEBACKER IN THE EARLY 1960s, THEN COACHED AND WAS AN ASSISTANT ATHLETICS DIRECTOR AT OU

"I just don't like 'em. *I don't like orange. Either shade. Period."* —FORMER OU TIGHT END TRENT SMITH, REFERRING TO TEXAS AND OKLAHOMA STATE

"Dominated 'em. Totally. Offense and defense. Beginning to end." —BARRY SWITZER AFTER OU's 17–7 WIN OVER NEBRASKA IN 1987, IN GAME OF THE CENTURY II

"OU's tradition is a vehicle. Once they got Bob Stoops, they were going to turn it around." —SWITZER ON OU's RENAISSANCE UNDER STOOPS

"Texas was our breakout game. Kansas State showed how tough we were. *Definitely, Nebraska showed the whole country OU was for real."* —FORMER OU OFFENSIVE LINEMAN FRANK ROMERO ON THE SOONERS' OCTOBER 2000 RUN EN ROUTE TO THE NATIONAL CHAMPIONSHIP

"He's like smoke through a keyhole." —FORMER TEXAS COACH DARRELL ROYAL, DESCRIBING OU HALFBACK JOE WASHINGTON

"Oklahoma knew when game day came around. You knew you were in a fistfight all day long. That's what Coach Stoops has brought back. Obviously, they have great schemes and very talented players, but what they do now is you'd better come ready to play or you're going to get embarrassed." —NORTH TEXAS COACH DARRELL DICKEY, A FORMER KANSAS STATE STANDOUT

"We play football and never get enough." —LAST LINE OF THE SOONER ROOTERS' OKLAHOMA YELL CARD FROM 1910

"He just took this team from the depths of college football and brought it to the very top again." —FORMER OU DEFENSIVE TACKLE JEREMY WILSON-GUEST, DESCRIBING THE IMPACT OF QUARTERBACK JOSH HEUPEL

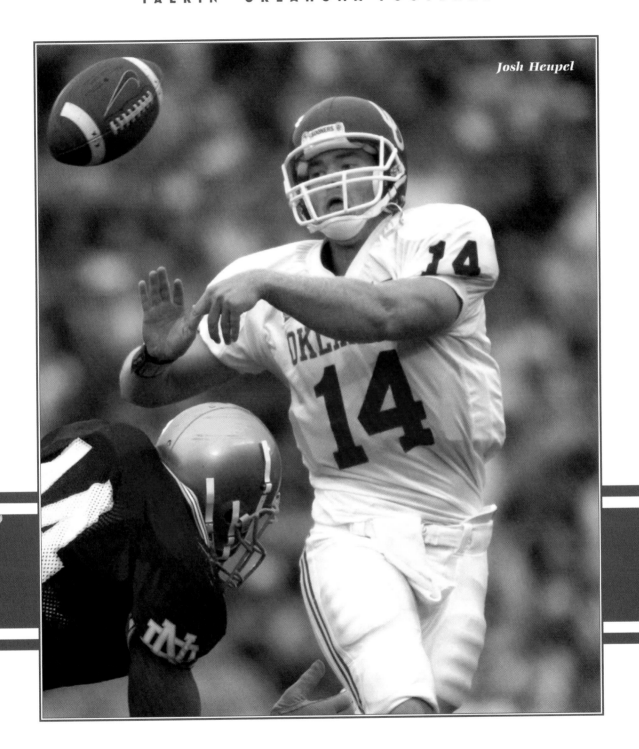

Josh Heupel

Jackie Shipp

"OU's winning tradition will never be entrusted to the timid or the weak."

—MESSAGE ON A SIGN THAT HUNG ON A WALL IN THE OU FOOTBALL OFFICES DURING THE 1970s AND 1980s

"You could have played that game without any fans, in an oil field in Oklahoma or a corn field in Nebraska, and you'd still have yourself a heck of a football game."

—OU DEFENSIVE LINE COACH AND FORMER PLAYER JACKIE SHIPP ON THE RIVALRY WITH NEBRASKA

"You don't realize what you're doing at the time. We just went out and beat people every weekend and thought that was the norm. We never really thought about it much."

—FORMER OU HALFBACK CLENDON THOMAS, ON THE SOONERS' NCAA-RECORD 47-GAME WINNING STREAK

"I've never been one of those crazy guys. It's just that people have an impression that the Boz lives 24-7. Once the game was over, Mr. Hyde was gone and Dr. Jekyll came out." —FORMER OU LINEBACKER BRIAN BOSWORTH

"It's a real fun game to play because everyone's so intense and when you score and make big plays, you love to celebrate, because half the stadium hates you." —FORMER OU QUARTERBACK NATE HYBL ON OU-TEXAS IN THE COTTON BOWL

"I think you see it in the guys' eyes. The want-to and the effort, everything is there. Everything is there and everything is in place and everyone understands that they are going to have to do their job 100 percent in order to fulfill our goal of getting the golden hat." —FORMER FULLBACK J.D. RUNNELS, DESCRIBING THE SOONERS' FOCUS IN PRACTICE DURING TEXAS WEEK

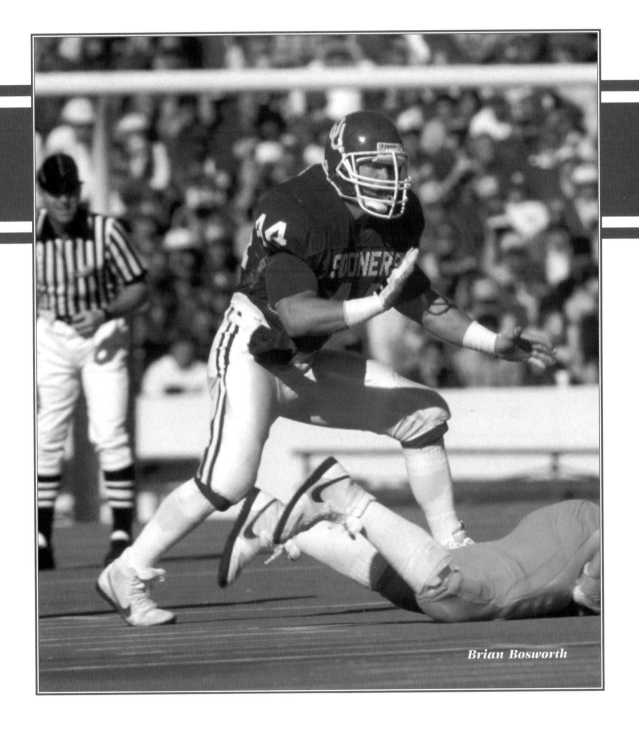

Brian Bosworth

Jason White

"Boomer!" —OU Heisman winner Billy Sims, in 2003, when Jason White became OU's fourth Heisman winner

"Sooner!" —White's reply to Sims on national television

"His teams dispelled the Dust Bowl Grapes of Wrath *image of the Depression years. They made Oklahoma proud and called national attention to the state's potential."* —former Oklahoma president George L. Cross on Bud Wilkinson's legacy

"We want to build a university the football team can be proud of." —former Oklahoma president George L. Cross, who hired Bud Wilkinson as head coach, to the Oklahoma state legislature when being asked why OU needed more funding

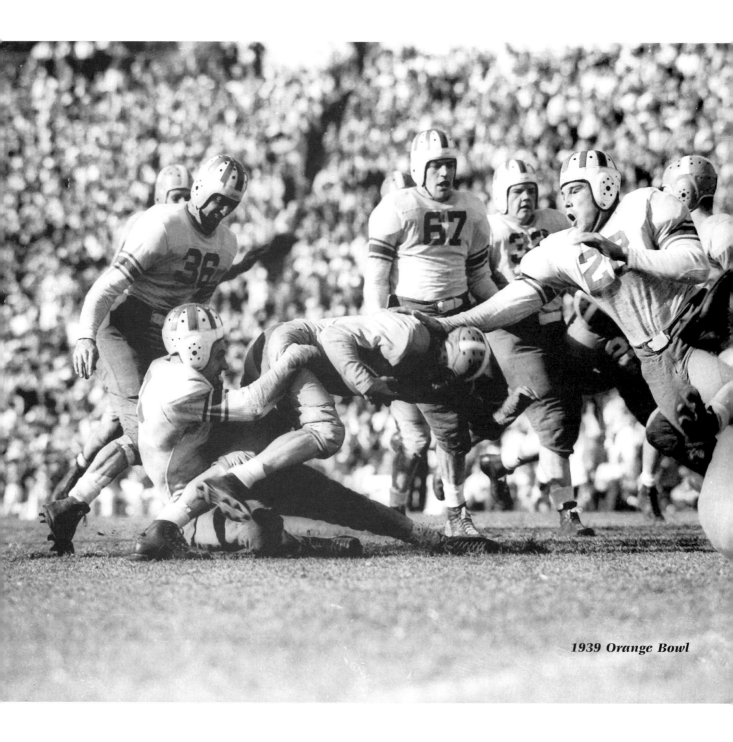

1939 Orange Bowl

FACTS AND FIGURES

Oklahoma has been one of college football's greatest postseason performers. In 39 postseason appearances, the Sooners have emerged victorious from 24 of them.

—— Bowl Tradition ——

RECORD: 24-14-1

1939 Orange Bowl	Tennessee 17, Oklahoma 0
1947 Gator Bowl	Oklahoma 34, NC State 13
1949 Sugar Bowl	Oklahoma 14, North Carolina 6
1950 Sugar Bowl	Oklahoma 35, LSU 0
1951 Sugar Bowl	Kentucky 13, Oklahoma 7
1954 Orange Bowl	Oklahoma 7, Maryland 0
1956 Orange Bowl	Oklahoma 20, Maryland 6
1958 Orange Bowl	Oklahoma 48, Duke 21
1959 Orange Bowl	Oklahoma 21, Syracuse 6
1963 Orange Bowl	Alabama 17, Oklahoma 0
1965 Gator Bowl	Florida State 36, Oklahoma 19
1968 Orange Bowl	Oklahoma 26, Tennessee 24

(continued on next page)

(continued)

1968 Bluebonnet Bowl	SMU 28, Oklahoma 27
1970 Bluebonnet Bowl	Oklahoma 24, Alabama 24
1972 Sugar Bowl	Oklahoma 40, Auburn 22
1973 Sugar Bowl	Oklahoma 14, Penn State 0
1976 Orange Bowl	Oklahoma 14, Michigan 6
1976 Fiesta Bowl	Oklahoma 41, Wyoming 7
1978 Orange Bowl	Arkansas 31, Oklahoma 6
1979 Orange Bowl	Oklahoma 31, Nebraska 24
1980 Orange Bowl	Oklahoma 24, Florida State 7
1981 Orange Bowl	Oklahoma 18, Florida State 17
1981 Sun Bowl	Oklahoma 40, Houston 14
1983 Fiesta Bowl	Arizona State 32, Oklahoma 21
1985 Orange Bowl	Washington 28, Oklahoma 17
1986 Orange Bowl	Oklahoma 25, Penn State 10
1987 Orange Bowl	Oklahoma 42, Arkansas 8
1988 Orange Bowl	Miami 20, Oklahoma 14
1989 Citrus Bowl	Clemson 13, Oklahoma 6
1991 Gator Bowl	Oklahoma 48, Virginia 14
1993 Hancock Bowl	Oklahoma 41, Texas Tech 10
1994 Copper Bowl	BYU 31, Oklahoma 6
1999 Independence Bowl	Ole Miss 27, Oklahoma 25
2001 Orange Bowl	Oklahoma 13, Florida State 2
2002 Cotton Bowl	Oklahoma 10, Arkansas 3
2003 Rose Bowl	Oklahoma 34, Washington State 14
2004 Sugar Bowl	LSU 21, Oklahoma 14
2005 Orange Bowl	USC 55, Oklahoma 19
2005 Holiday Bowl	Oklahoma 17, Oregon 14

Adrian Peterson is airborn going through the Oregon defense during the 2005 Holiday Bowl.

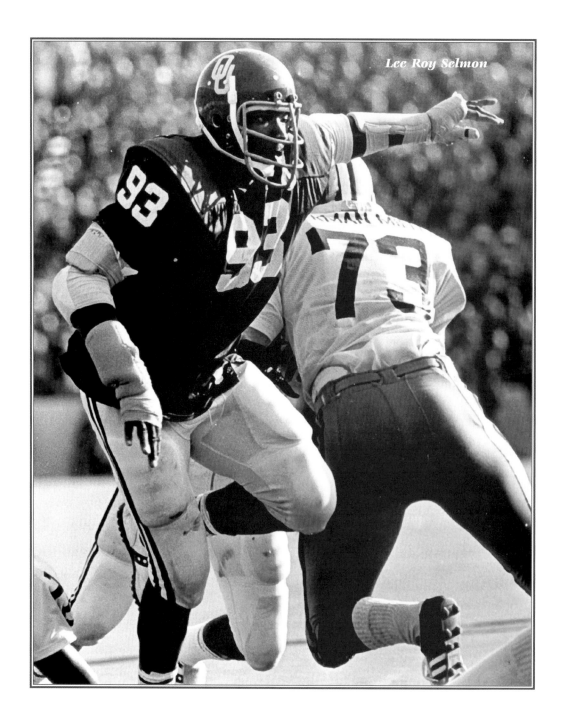

Lee Roy Selmon

—— Oklahoma ——
in the College Football Hall of Fame

NAME	POSITION	YEARS	INDUCTED
Kurt Burris	Center	1951–1954	2000
Tony Casillas	Middle Guard	1982–1985	2004
Forest Geyer	Fullback	1913–1915	1973
Keith Jackson	Tight End	1984–1987	2001
Tommy McDonald	Halfback	1954–1956	1985
Bennie Owen	Coach	1905–1926	1951
Jim Owens	End	1946–1949	1982
Steve Owens	Halfback	1967–1969	1991
Greg Pruitt	Halfback	1970–1972	1999
Claude Reeds	Fullback	1910–1913	1961
J.D. Roberts	Guard	1951–1953	1993
Lee Roy Selmon	Defensive Tackle	1972–1975	1988
Billy Sims	Halfback	1975–1979	1995
Barry Switzer	Coach	1973–1988	2001
Jerry Tubbs	Center	1954–1956	1996
Billy Vessels	Halfback	1950–1952	1974
Joe Washington	Running Back	1972–1975	2005
Jim Weatherall	Tackle	1948–1951	1992
Bud Wilkinson	Coach	1947–1963	1969
Waddy Young	End	1936–1938	1986

Jason White

136

Career Statistical Leaders

Rushes: 958, Steve Owens

Rushing Yards: 4,118, Billy Sims

Rushing Touchdowns: 57, Steve Owens

Yards per Attempt: 7.4, Greg Pruitt

All-Purpose Yards: 5,881, Joe Washington

Pass Attempts: 1,025, Josh Heupel

Pass Completions: 654, Josh Heupel

Passing Yards: 7,922, Jason White

Passing Touchdowns: 81, Jason White

Completion Percentage: 63.8, Josh Heupel

Receptions: 217, Mark Clayton

Receiving Yards: 3,220, Mark Clayton

Receiving Touchdowns: 31, Mark Clayton

Total Offense: 7,735, Jason White

Tackles: 530, Daryl Hunt

Tackles for Loss: 59, Rocky Calmus

Interceptions: 18, Darrell Royal

Sacks: 31.5, Cedric Jones

The National Championship Seasons

1950: 10-1

Coach: Bud Wilkinson

Captains: Harry Moore, Blackwell, Oklahoma; Norman McNabb, Norman, Oklahoma

September 30	Boston College	W	28–0
October 7	Texas A&M	W	34–28
October 14	Texas at Dallas	W	14–13
October 21	Kansas State	W	58–0
October 28	at Iowa State	W	20–7
November 4	at Colorado	W	27–18
November 11	at Kansas	W	33–13
November 18	Missouri	W	41–7
November 25	Nebraska	W	49–35
December 2	at Oklahoma State	W	41–14

Sugar Bowl

| January 1 | Kentucky | L | 7–13 |

Statistical Leaders

Rushing: Billy Vessels, 870 yards, 15 TDs

Passing: Claude Arnold, 1,048 yards, 13 TDs

Receiving: Billy Vessels, 11 rec., 229 yards, 2 TDs

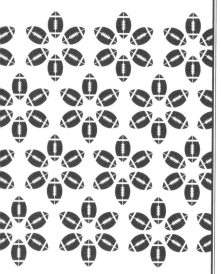

1955: 11-0

Coach: Bud Wilkinson

Captains: Bo Bolinger, Muskogee, Oklahoma; Cecil Morris, Lawton, Oklahoma; Bob Loughridge, Poteau, Oklahoma

September 24	at North Carolina	W	13–6
October 1	Pittsburgh	W	26–14
October 8	Texas at Dallas	W	20–0
October 15	Kansas	W	44–6
October 22	Colorado	W	56–21
October 29	at Kansas State	W	40–7
November 5	at Missouri	W	20–0
November 12	Iowa State	W	52–0
November 19	at Nebraska	W	41–0
November 26	Oklahoma State	W	53–0

Orange Bowl

January 1	Maryland	W	20–6

Statistical Leaders

Rushing: Tommy McDonald, 702 yards, 14 TDs

Passing: Tommy McDonald, 265 yards, 0 TDs

Receiving: Joe Mobra, 6 rec., 128 yards, 1 TD

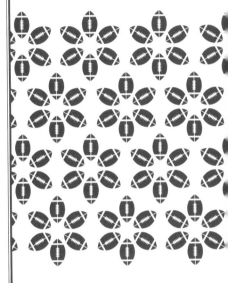

1956: 10-0

Coach: Bud Wilkinson

Captains: Ed Gray, Odessa, Texas; Jerry Tubbs, Breckenridge, Texas

September 29	North Carolina	W	36–0
October 6	Kansas State	W	66–0
October 13	Texas at Dallas	W	45–0
October 20	at Kansas	W	34–12
October 27	at Notre Dame	W	40–0
November 3	at Colorado	W	27–19
November 10	at Iowa State	W	44–0
November 17	Missouri	W	67–14
November 24	Nebraska	W	54–6
December 1	at Oklahoma State	W	53–0

Statistical Leaders

Rushing: Tommy McDonald, 853 yards, 12 TDs

Passing: Jimmy Harris, 482 yards, 8 TDs

Receiving: Tommy McDonald, 12 rec., 282 yards, 4 TDs

1974: 11-0

Coach: Barry Switzer

Captains: Steve Davis, Sallisaw, Oklahoma; Kyle Davis, Altus, Oklahoma; Rod Shoate, Spiro, Oklahoma; Randy Hughes, Tulsa, Oklahoma

September 14	Baylor	W	28–11
September 28	Utah State	W	72–3
October 5	Wake Forest	W	63–0
October 12	Texas at Dallas	W	16–13
October 19	at Colorado	W	49–14
October 26	Kansas State	W	63–0
November 2	at Iowa State	W	28–10
November 9	Missouri	W	37–0
November 16	at Kansas	W	45–14
November 23	at Nebraska	W	28–14
November 30	Oklahoma State	W	44–13

Statistical Leaders

Rushing: Joe Washington, 1,321 yards, 13 TDs

Passing: Steve Davis, 601 yards, 11 TDs

Receiving: Tinker Owens, 18 rec., 413 yards, 5 TDs

1975: 11-1

Coach: Barry Switzer

Captains: Lee Roy Selmon, Eufala, Oklahoma; Dewey Selmon, Eufala, Oklahoma; Joe Washington, Port Arthur, Texas; Steve Davis, Sallisaw, Oklahoma

September 13	Oregon	W	62–7
September 20	Pittsburgh	W	46–10
September 26	at Miami	W	20–17
October 4	Colorado	W	21–20
October 11	Texas at Dallas	W	24–17
October 18	at Kansas State	W	25–3
October 25	Iowa State	W	39–7
November 1	at Oklahoma State	W	27–7
November 8	Kansas	L	3–23
November 15	at Missouri	W	28–27
November 22	Nebraska	W	35–10

Orange Bowl

January 1	Michigan	W	14–6

Statistical Leaders

Rushing: Joe Washington, 871 yards, 11 TDs

Passing: Steve Davis, 438 yards, 1 TD

Receiving: Tinker Owens, 9 rec., 241 yards, 1 TD

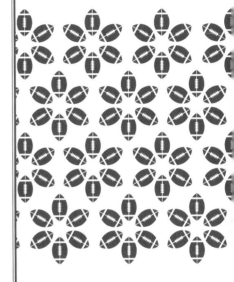

1985: 10-1

Coach: Barry Switzer

Captains: Tony Casillas, Tulsa, Oklahoma; Kevin Murphy, Richardson, Texas; Eric Pope, Seminole, Oklahoma

September 28	at Minnesota	W	13–7
October 5	at Kansas State	W	41–6
October 12	Texas at Dallas	W	14–7
October 19	Miami	L	14–27
October 26	Iowa State	W	59–14
November 2	Kansas	W	48–6
November 9	at Missouri	W	51–6
November 16	Colorado	W	31–0
November 23	Nebraska	W	27–7
November 30	at Oklahoma State	W	13–0
December 7	SMU	W	35–13

Orange Bowl

January 1	Penn State	W	25–10

Statistical Leaders

Rushing: Jamelle Holieway, 861 yards, 8 TDs

Passing: Jamelle Holieway, 517 yards, 5 TDs

Receiving: Keith Jackson, 20 rec., 486 yards, 2 TDs

2000: 13-0

Coach: Bob Stoops

Captains: Josh Heupel, Aberdeen, South Dakota; Seth Littrell, Muskogee, Oklahoma; Chris Hammons, Sulphur, Oklahoma; Rocky Calmus, Jenks, Oklahoma; Torrance Marshall, Miami, Florida; Bubba Burcham, Mustang, Oklahoma

September 2	UTEP	W	55–14
September 9	Arkansas State	W	45–7
September 23	Rice	W	42–14
September 30	Kansas	W	34–16
October 7	Texas at Dallas	W	63–14
October 14	at Kansas State	W	41–31
October 28	Nebraska	W	31–14
November 4	at Baylor	W	56–7
November 11	at Texas A&M	W	35–31
November 18	Texas Tech	W	27–13
November 25	at Oklahoma State	W	12–7
December 2	Kansas State	W	27–24

Orange Bowl

January 3	Florida State	W	13–2

Statistical Leaders

Rushing: Quentin Griffin, 696 yards, 16 TDs

Passing: Josh Heupel, 3,172 yards, 18 TDs

Receiving: Antwone Savage, 47 rec., 594 yards, 3 TDs